To Daphne

from Cousin Derek

Our next meeting must be much quicker than 50 years between–

All Love

MANAGING PURCHASING

MANAGING PURCHASING

ORGANIZING, PLANNING AND CONTROL

BRIAN FARRINGTON, PhD, MSc, BSc, FCIPS

DEREK W.F. WATERS FCIPS

CHAPMAN & HALL

University and Professional Division

London · Glasgow · New York · Tokyo · Melbourne · Madras

Published by Chapman & Hall, 2–6 Boundary Row, London SE1 8HN, UK

Chapman & Hall, 2–6 Boundary Row, London SE1 8HN, UK

Blackie Academic & Professional, Wester Cleddens Road, Bishopbriggs, Glasgow G64 2NZ, UK

Chapman & Hall, One Penn Plaza, 41st Floor, New York NY10119, USA

Chapman & Hall Japan, Thomson Publishing Japan, Hirakawacho Nemoto Building, 6F, 1–7–11 Hirakawa-cho, Chiyoda-ku, Tokyo 102, Japan

Chapman & Hall Australia, Thomas Nelson Australia, 102 Dodds Street, South Melbourne, Victoria 3205, Australia

Chapman & Hall India, R. Seshadri, 32 Second Main Road, CIT East, Madras 600 035, India

First edition 1994

Typeset in 11/13pt Bembo by Photoprint, Torquay, Devon
Printed in Great Britain by Clays Ltd, St Ives plc

ISBN 0 412 56760 1

A catalogue record for this book is available from the British Library

Library of Congress Cataloging-in-Publication data available

Printed on permanent acid-free text paper, manufactured in accordance with the proposed ANSI/NISO Z 39.48–199X and ANSI Z 39.48–1984

CONTENTS

PREFACE

As soon as Humans decided that specialization was the route to the efficient development of resources, the buyer and the seller made their appearance on the world's stage.

The battle to obtain adequate supply has always been competitive. Often the difference between winning and losing a war depended on who won the battle for supply.

The supply manager of today is competing just as determinedly as ever. Not only are there domestic competitors, there are also competitors in a dozen countries or more, trying to obtain reliable supply at a better price in order to put him or her out of business.

The best-equipped and the best-led purchasing departments will be the ones who decide who stays in business and who goes to the wall.

This book reviews and explains the methods, tools and techniques which are necessary to ensure that the supply battle is won. In order to get down to basics, it assumes that the reader has just started in purchasing management, but it is of equal value to experienced purchasing managers who want to review their skills. It is also a valuable addition to the library of the buyer who aspires to purchasing management.

GLOSSARY OF TERMS USED IN PURCHASING

Advance payment
A payment made to a supplier, usually sent with the purchase order, prior to work commencing on a project or prior to manufacture starting.

Amortization
A process under which a supplier recovers the cost of dies, tooling etc., over an agreed quantity of components. During this period of time the title to the dies, tooling etc. remains that of the supplier.

Arbitration
An alternative process to the courts used to resolve contractual differences which arise during or after contract performance. The source of arbitration should be agreed at time of placing purchase order.

Bank guarantee
A legal document issued by a bank or insurance company which places an obligation upon them to pay the amount of the guarantee in the event of specified terms of default by the supplier; often required when advance payments are made.

Bid bond
A financial undertaking given by the bidder, through a bank or insurance company, that is forfeited to the buying company in the event that a bid is withdrawn prior to the buyer's acceptance. This is always providing that such acceptance takes place within the bid validity period.

Cartel
An association of companies producing the same or similar commodities. While each one retains their independent existence the cartel formulates plans and policies to control and stabilize sales and prices, in their interest.

Cash flow
The rate at which a business uses cash to support its operations. If excessive inventory exists it requires funding through cash, as does work in progress. It is to the benefit of a business if it can increase its use of cash.

Caveat emptor
A Latin term meaning 'Let the buyer beware'. In essence it points out the important role played by buying staff when a contract is being negotiated and awarded. The onus is upon the buyer to ensure that the contract reflects the buyer's wishes.

Contract master file
A comprehensive file that contains all correspondence and contractual detail, no matter which department generates it, with regard to a particular contract. It should be kept for the statutory period associated with the Companies Act.

Contractual risk
The degree of exposure that exists for the buyer in a contractual relationship with a supplier. If the supplier's terms and conditions of sale have been accepted, the risk will be high for the buyer.

Cost analysis
A detailed approach to evaluating the seller's cost elements within a proposed price. This uses the data provided in a cost breakdown and relates them, wherever possible, to cost information in the possession of the buyer.

Cost avoidance
This expression is used to show savings made against the successful resistance of price increase claims from suppliers.

Cost breakdown
A detailed explanation of the cost elements that have contributed to the supplier's proposed selling price. This would usually be detailed

in terms of materials, labour, overheads (fixed and variable) and profit.

Cost in use
A summation of all costs that will be incurred in the long-term use of a product or component. This will include spares, maintenance, servicing, repair etc. All of these costs will need assessing at the time of purchasing the product or component. This term is sometimes referred to as 'full life cost'.

Cost reduction
This term refers to savings made against a cost reduction programme which would include resourcing, change in specification, change in delivery method, use of new tooling etc.

Critical path analysis
A system of planning activities necessary for the completion on time of a project or manufacture of a complex product. When the activities are mapped out the critical path is revealed. Usually this system is referred to as CPA.

Demurrage
A charge paid for detaining a vehicle either collecting or delivering goods beyond the period of charter originally agreed or for delaying a ship by failing to unload on time.

Determination
A legal expression which means to bring the contract to an end. In many contracts this is referred to as cancellation. In either event the buyer may be faced with costs if the buyer cancels. The basis of these costs should be defined in the contract.

Discount
A reduction in the purchase price, usually a percentage of the price, offered by the supplier in return for specified quantity purchases or other contractual obligation.

Dutch auction
A process which is not permitted within most buying companies whereby one seller is played off against others. During this process the buyer reveals other sellers' prices and persistently calls meetings to seek further reductions in price. This is an unprofessional practice and is not recommended.

Electronic data interchange
Often using the designatory letters EDI, this is a system of electronic communication between buyer and seller which enables them to respond quickly to the needs of the buyer's business. It can mean accessing the supplier's inventory, with automatic ordering through linked computers.

Escrow
A legal term referring to a deed which becomes effective on the operation of a future event. It is commonly used on computer software contracts to obtain source codes in the event that the supplier goes into liquidation.

Expediting
A systematic approach by the buying company aimed at ensuring that the supplier will meet a contracted delivery date.

Firm price
A price agreed at the time of contract placement which will remain unchanged throughout the contract period.

Fixed price
A price which is fixed at the time of contract placement, but which may change in the contract period in line with an agreed formula which involves pre-agreed indices.

Force majeure
A contractual expression through which the supplier can have, within the contract, legitimate reasons for delayed delivery. It would include such matters as strikes, lock-outs, acts of God, fire etc. All such reasons must be considered for legitimacy within a specified contract.

Free issue
This refers to materials which are the property of the buying company which are sent to the supplier for incorporation into their product. It may also refer to items sent for machining which are owned by the buying company.

Handing-over certificate
A document used to cover the transfer of responsibility for newly installed plant and equipment from the seller to the buyer. It is not a contractual document but carries important legal significance.

INCOTERMS
An acronym for international commercial terms used in contracts for sale of goods in international markets. It contains various terms which define the respective obligations upon buyer and seller. A booklet of INCOTERMS is available from the International Chamber of Commerce. The latest issue is dated 1990 (correct at time of going to press).

Instruction to proceed
A verbal or written instruction to a supplier to proceed with contractual work, issued prior to the formal contract. Often referred to as an ITP it does create a legal relationship between the buyer and the seller. It is the specific wording that will distinguish it from a letter of intent (defined below).

Intellectual property rights
Rights vested in the holder for intellectual effort in design, original thought, invention etc., which confer rights on the holder. If these rights are breached by the buyer the holder has remedies in law for infringement. It is important to relate this to the Copyright, Designs and Patents Act 1988.

Just in time
A contractual arrangement wherein the supplier makes deliveries to the buyer's premises at a precise time to match production or project needs. It avoids high levels of inventory and has cash flow benefits.

Lead time
The total elapsed time from identifying a need to having the product or component available for use in the buying company. The accuracy of defining lead time will directly affect inventory levels and reliability in contracting for deliveries.

Learning curve
A technique for assessing the direct linkage between the time taken to undertake a task and the quantity produced. When high amounts of labour are required there will be reductions in time taken, hence there is an impact on price.

Liquidated damages
An agreed contractual remedy whereby, typically, the buyer deducts fixed percentages from the contract value for each defined period of

time that the supplier is late on delivery. Such deductions must be genuine pre-estimates of loss.

Letter of intent
A communication from the buyer to the seller informing the latter that it is the intention to place a contract for that which is the subject of a quotation. If correctly worded it does not create a legal relationship. See definition of instructions to proceed above.

Lowest ultimate cost
This requires the buyer to take into account the cost of purchase as well as spares, maintenance, use of energy, life of product, obsolescence etc.

Material requirement planning (MRP)
A process to plan the availability of stock to satisfy the demands of products in a given period.

Material resource planning (MRPII)
A process to plan production and establish lead times based on consideration of available machine/production time and manufacturing cycle time.

Negotiation
The process for resolving differences of opinion which arise in contract dealings between buyer and seller. The legitimate process of negotiation is not to be confused with a 'Dutch auction'.

Non-recurring cost
Costs which are incurred by the seller in fulfilling a contractual obligation, but which only occur once, usually at the outset of a contract. Examples would be jigs, fixtures, design, software writing etc. These costs are negotiable and there is no contractual obligation upon the buyer to pay them unless agreed in the contract.

Official Journal of the European Community
This is usually abbreviated to OJEC. It is the official journal of the European Community in which potential contracts in excess of a defined value are advertised.

Penalty clause
This is illegal in English law. The buyer is not allowed to hold the

supplier *in terrorem* (in terror). The term is often misused to signify liquidated damages, which does not mean the same thing.

Performance bond
This is a contractual undertaking by either a bank or insurance company to the buying company to pay a defined sum of money in the event that the supplier does not meet a contractual obligation. A company standard document exists within most organizations to meet this purpose.

Price variation formulae
A contractual mechanism which provides for the movement of price during the contract period. Usually consisting of three elements, fixed, labour and material expressed in a formula. The latter two are linked to defined indices.

Procurement cycle
The phases that will be passed through by procurement specialists before, during and after contract formation to ensure that all aspects of a purchase have been dealt with. These phases involve time elapse which must be considered within the product, service or project lead time.

Product liability
Legislation now exists throughout the EC which requires manufacturers to accept responsibility for the safe performance of the products they manufacture and supply.

Product support
The activities provided by the supplier after the product has been commissioned and handed over to the buyer. This will include the availability of spares and engineers for a specified period of time.

Progress payments
Agreed sums of monies paid by the buyer to the seller during product manufacture or project work. These sums must be linked to demonstrable work packages completed and title in the goods must pass to the buyer when such payments are made. The overall payment package is often called a payment schedule.

Purchase research
An activity undertaken by procurement to ensure the supplier's

organization, pricing, finances etc. are adequately researched prior to placing contracts or undertaking contract negotiation.

Quotation analysis
The process of listing all relevant factors to be assessed when quotations are submitted and then ranking them for contract importance. The listing should include all relevant technical and commercial factors.

Rebate
An amount repaid by the seller, typically one year in arrears (although this can be negotiated), to the buyer when purchases have reached a pre-agreed sum of money or number of units. The amount and method of payment is negotiable.

Return on capital employed
A measure of company profitability which relates profits to the amount of capital utilized in a business.

Shelf life
Some items will deteriorate in storage after a certain time has elapsed. This is known as shelf life and must be identified. It requires that stock rotation is properly managed and that there is agreed responsibility for identifying goods with restricted shelf life.

Supplier appraisal
A methodology used at the pre-contract award phase to assess the supplier's capabilities to undertake defined work. It will involve quality, safety, commercial and financial evaluation of a supplier.

Supplier partnerships
A relationship between a buying company and a supplier whereby both parties agree to develop a long-term, often exclusive, relationship to the mutual benefit of both parties.

Supplier quality assurance
A systematic approach to evaluating a supplier's capability to manage quality through all phases of purchase, handling, manufacture etc. The system should be independent of procurement.

Supplier rationalization
A strategic approach used by the buyer with the express purpose of reducing the existing number of suppliers to more manageable

proportions, from which various contractual benefits will be obtained.

Tenders
Formal requests, or invitations, issued by the buyer for the seller to make an offer to sell (the tender) against strict conditions regarding submission dates, opening, negotiation, validity periods etc. The unqualified acceptance by the buyer of a tender will create a contract.

Total quality management
The process of managing all aspects of quality from specification development, through the supplier's manufacturing process, inspection, testing and acceptance criteria.

Unliquidated damages
These are amounts of monies paid by the seller to the buyer which reflect the actual losses sustained by the buyer in the event of contract default by the seller. These are more commonly referred to as consequential loss.

Validity period
The time specified by the bidder during which the offer will remain valid, in other words open for acceptance by the buyer. At the end of this specified period the offer lapses unless it is extended by the seller.

Value analysis
A systematic approach to investigating all aspects of cost and eliminating unnecessary cost in a manufactured product, after production has commenced.

Value engineering
A systematic review of all projected costs within a product, conducted at the design and engineering phase of product life.

Value for money
The situation that exists when the buyer has obtained from the supplier optimum cost in respect of the total features of a purchase. It avoids a fixation with price and requires that all aspects of cost are studied with care.

Variation order
An amendment to a contract instructing the supplier to undertake

additional work or to omit some work already authorized, and stating the impact on price and other contract terms.

Vendor rating
A systematic approach to monitoring and measuring aspects of a supplier's contractual performance, including delivery, quantity, quality, service support etc.

Without prejudice
A legal term meaning without dismissing or detracting from an existing right or claim. It can refer to informal discussions which are seeking to resolve a contractual dispute.

Zero defects
This refers to the supply of goods by a supplier where there are no faulty items within a delivery. The onus is upon the supplier for quality management and associated control of quality when delivering.

1

THE 10 BASIC QUESTIONS

No doubt when you were given responsibility for Purchasing by the MD, you were also given a pep-talk and told what great confidence the company had in you.

THE DIRECTIVE

You were also given, in broad terms, an outline of the expectation for your achievements in your new role. Probabilities being what they are, you made a note (before you forgot any of it) of the main objectives which were as follows.

1. Supply must be improved. Production lines are often stopped due to late deliveries of raw materials, components and capital equipment, and purchasing must rectify this situation urgently.
2. Quality control report that there is a high percentage of deliveries made to the factory which they have to reject back to the supplier. The knock-on effect of these rejections influences production and purchasing must correct this situation quickly.
3. Our budgets for new capital equipment are growing annually and there is clear evidence that we are paying too much for what we buy. Purchasing must find ways to control this expenditure and make sure that we get value for money.
4. Finance/Accounting are concerned that our material costs are rising due to price increases being conceded to suppliers and is threatening our profit margins to the extent that redundancies may have to be called for. Purchasing ought to be able to reduce costs urgently.
5. Our consumable costs and non-production purchases appear high. Purchasing should be able to reduce them.

6. Purchasing are our biggest spenders, and the costs of our material budget and inventory are a constant threat to our cash flow situation. Purchasing should be able to mitigate these problems speedily.
7. We've been in difficulties lately with some expensive law suits due to our being 'found against' in legal actions over contracts with some of our suppliers. Purchasing should be able to provide (with assistance from our own legal people) 100% protection in the future for the company.

No doubt the other note you made was the MD's remark that results were expected to be seen within, let us say, six months! The final shot was that you had either to form a department from scratch, or near scratch, to staff the purchasing function!

Sitting in your office a few hours later when the euphoria has evaporated, leaving a cold clammy hand gripping the intestines and thinking furiously through the 'How, Why, When and What' of the company's problems, it is as well to keep in mind what purchasing is.

THE PURCHASING DEPARTMENT'S ROLE

It is a machine for deploying money in exchange for goods and services at the lowest ultimate cost. Like any other machine, it needs managing and controlling. Ideally, the manager should be a formally trained buyer, but even a promoted buyer's buying skills will not be very much help in the early months of the new position as the new manager has to learn to manage. On the other hand the manager coming from some other discipline has management skills, but will have to acquire buying skills. But from whichever route the new manager has come, the new incumbent has a lot to learn and learn fast!

THE DEFINITION OF LOWEST ULTIMATE COST

It is a fact that buyers expect the boss to be a top gun buyer eventually; but their prime need will be for positive direction which you must provide.

For many years, buyers were taught that it was their job to procure the right material:

at the right time;

at the right quality;
at the right quantity;
to the right place;
at the right price.

These are known as the 'Five Rights' – although there are actually Six Rights!

It's not a bad starting point but, over the last few years, the concept of lowest ultimate cost has emerged to amplify the Five Rights.

The difference between the two objectives lies in focus. The reality is that the cost of a component starts in design engineering. Traditionally, the designers will want to specify the supplier to be used on the most critical items. Unless purchasing are involved and taking an effective hand in the choice of the specified supplier, the company will be (or can be) committed to the use of a supplier who is an embarrassment to purchasing in one or other of the Five Rights.

SOURCE SELECTION

The selection of the right supplier is, or should be, entirely a purchasing responsibility. Areas where traditionally 'amateur buyers' in other departments seek to carry out this role are also likely to choose suppliers that a properly constituted purchasing department wouldn't touch with a barge pole! Sooner or later those departments will have to give up this role to purchasing which will give them more time to get on with their own job.

The supply and quality performance of the suppliers is a function of good supply source selection, which is again a purchasing function.

Once the finished product goes through the door to the customer, the buyers' responsibility does not finish, as most think it does.

Warranty claims cost money since replacement is free, so it is still purchasing's responsibility to ensure quality.

So, let us imagine that the buyer is satisfied with the unit price being paid – how much inventory does the buyer need to carry? Inventory is a dreadful waste of money if the suppliers are good – yet it is an aspect of lowest ultimate cost which is often overlooked. If the reason for the high inventory is that the supplier is inefficient, then the answer is obvious. So, lowest ultimate cost is the objective, and demands a wider range of activity and responsibility than the Five Rights used to do.

The objectives given by the boss at your promotion interview are each aspects of achieving lowest ultimate cost and clearly the boss is expecting considerable and fast improvement.

It is now your responsibility to attempt to quantify the problems in order that you can start to address the various tasks which have to be undertaken.

You will no doubt be aware of the slogan 'Every department in a company is both a customer and a seller to every other department'. Purchasing are actually very big customers of many departments but, at the moment, our interest is in the departments who are our customers and a trawl around the 'customers' to obtain the answers to the 10 questions is our first step in quantifying the task.

THE 10 BASIC QUESTIONS

Because purchasing is a fiscal department, one aspect to which the purchasing manager has to pay very great attention is the cost of purchases. This sector will receive considerable attention in the following chapters and the first questions which need rapid answers are those directed to Finance/Accounting. In some companies, the roles are combined in one department and in others they are separate, but between the two functions you will get your answers.

1. The first question is a request for a list, or a tab which shows all the suppliers used in the last 12 months listed in descending order of annual spend.
2. The second question is what is the company breakdown of the ratios of material, labour and overhead?
3. What percentage of goods received are invoiced at a different price than the one on the order – necessitating an account query. Do all goods received pass through goods receiving? (Don't forget to request a list of offenders.)
4. How are suppliers paid?
   (a) 30 days from receipt of invoice?
   (b) 45 days from end of month in which the goods are received?
   (c) Other?

The answers that you receive will provide you with a good 30% of the management information you need to plan to improve profit, organize your department and to control your staff.

The next department to visit is quality control (QC).

The boss said that incoming quality problems were unacceptably high so your questions to quality control are as follows.

5. How are incoming goods inspected? Their reply will probably be within a range of methods which will include the following.
   (a) Inspection at suppliers' premises.
   (b) A statistical plan where a small number of batches are selected for inspection and, from these, depending on quantity per batch, a small sample is taken and tested. If there are rejects found which are greater than the statistical plan, the batch is rejected.
   (c) One hundred per cent inspection. All rejects are thrown out and the balance passed for production.
   (d) Varying levels of inspection are probable, e.g. life and limb, or safety items, are inspected much more thoroughly than less important items.
   (e) Supplier Assurance. This is an agreement between the supplier and the company that all deliveries will have been tested at source and there is no need for inspection by the customer. Purchasing need to raise a contract which defines supplier responsibility in case rejects do get passed through the process and result in extra cost to The Company. The Company agrees with the supplier that periodic random audits by company QC personnel will take place to ensure that the supplier is adhering to all the necessary procedures to ensure that quality remains high at the supplier.

   You should request a list of the suppliers by Inspection Category.
6. The second request to QC is for a list of the worst offenders in terms of batches supplied and rejects incurred over a suitable period (a year for preference – but the last six months is vital).

On then to Manufacturing and Assembly, who are your most vociferous customers and your most outspoken critics, so you will be excused if you feel that you are putting your head in the lion's mouth – but treat them well and they will become your closest allies.

Firstly, you need to know how they produce the product(s). This isn't a question but a mini teach-in.

It is axiomatic that Purchasing must know the materials they buy, what they look like etc., and how the components are used and the end products on which they are fitted.

Is the production flow or batch, or one-off?

The material supply required to supply these different production cycles is considerably different and since Purchasing is the spokesperson for manufacturing and assembly in terms of supply, it is imperative to know how manufacturing works.

- Flow line production requires regular top-up deliveries so that each time the operator turns round for the next component to fit, it's there to hand, waiting to be fitted.
- Batch production requires normally a full kit of components to be marshalled and issued to manufacturing and assembly complete, and ready for the subsequent processes.
- One-off production is often run in a similar method to batch production except that material is scheduled in line with need, i.e. if a ship is being built, the steel for the hull is required perhaps a year before the radar is needed – so delivery dates are staged.

The question to put to Assembly/Manufacturing is as follows.

7. I would like a list of all your most troublesome shortages – which are often repeated – and the suppliers who cause these problems.

   There are only three causes for delivery date promises to be broken (apart from acts of God, strikes at the suppliers, or fires). They are:

   (a) rejected materials found too late to be replaced in time to maintain the required date;
   (b) late delivery by a supplier to a pre-agreed schedule;
   (c) bad scheduling where the material has been called off too late for the supplier to be able to react in time to meet the required date.

Purchasing can take action to prevent all three of these causes of loss of production and the methods to prevent them will be discussed in the following chapters.

The next port of call is Production Control, whose role is to receive the orders from customers obtained via Sales/Marketing and by a method akin to critical path analysis to co-ordinate all departments to produce the product in line with the promise given by Sales/Marketing to the customer. The system they use can vary from manual sequencing (becoming very rare) through to various material requirement planning (MRP) systems. The result is the same, which is:

- to trigger off material deliveries to arrive in time for production to manufacture to time;
- to instruct Manufacturing/Assembly to leave windows at each machine to allow the material to be slotted in for the requisite operations in the most economic method;

- to instruct shipping to organize transport to be available when the goods are ready.

And so on. Hopefully, every step in their plan/strategy works – but none of it has a hope if the material is not available when required.

The eighth question concerns lead times. To make a complicated casting can easily take four months from receipt of the order at your chosen suppliers, while a standard bolt is available within a day.

Therefore, we refer to a four-month 'lead time' for the casting and a one-day 'lead time' for the bolt, but clearly the casting is the controlling factor in deciding when machining of the casting can take place.

So question 8 is posed in two parts, as follows.

8. (a) What lead time for delivery do Sales/Marketing offer to our customers (assuming we only build to order and our longest lead is 16 weeks?
   (b) How long from receipt of order does it take Production Control to trigger off Purchasing, once the order is received?

A typical answer to such a question will be: 'Normally Sales/ Marketing offer delivery in 20 weeks which gives Manufacturing 4 weeks to manufacture and assemble – but business being what it is, they often promise 16 weeks so we request delivery in 12 weeks of the necessary materials. As regards the time it takes us to plan and schedule production from receipt of order, it varies between one and two weeks.'

The reply to question 8 shows that The Company contributes to its own shortage problems – but it is up to Purchasing to find ways round this problem and the methods available will be discussed in later chapters.

The visit to Sales/Marketing requires the answers to two questions which should be capable of being answered by Sales/Marketing, but may have to be referred back to Finance.

9. What is the mark-up applied to works cost which we charge the supplier for our products?
10. Since the material cost is the highest percentage of contribution to works cost, Purchasing can vary prices by conceding to price requests, thus reducing profit unless The Company puts up its prices to the customer. Or, it can reduce prices by negotiation, resourcing etc. In the latter case, what would Sales/Marketing do? Would they pass on the reduction to the customer in order to sell more product – or would they keep the price the same and improve profit?

This question may seem naïve, except for the fact that if Sales/Marketing decided to increase sales at a lower price, you could be embarrassed by not having the capacity available to meet the upswing in production.

Also, if the normal margin over works cost is, for example, 10%, the margin is very vulnerable to any price increases you may have to concede. Surprisingly, this link is often very badly maintained and the first Purchasing hears about the loss of profit is from Finance when the damage has been done. But if Purchasing stays on its toes – the problem can be handled safely.

THE ANSWERS TO THE 10 BASIC QUESTIONS

The 10 basic questions have provoked the responses which will provide you with many of your major sources of actions over the next year.

If we start by examining the answers to questions 1 to 4 which were the Finance-directed questions, we find that their answers were as follows.

Question 1

Total turnover over the last 12 months: £25 000 000.

Of the top 70 suppliers who account for £21 000 000, e.g. 80% of the total spend, the breakdown is listed in supplier order but, for simplicity, an initial grouping has been done.

Castings	2 000 000	10 suppliers
Pressings	3 000 000	5 suppliers
Electrics/electronics	7 000 000	19 suppliers
Utilities:		
Gas, water and electricity	1 000 000	3 suppliers
Rubber mouldings	1 000 000	3 suppliers
Forgings	1 000 000	6 suppliers
Standard parts	2 000 000	11 suppliers
Paint	1 000 000	4 suppliers
Copper	1 000 000	3 suppliers
Steel	2 000 000	6 suppliers
Total	£21 000 000	70 suppliers
All other requirements	4 000 000	1130 suppliers
Grand total	£25 000 000	1200 suppliers

It will be seen that 70 suppliers share 80% of the total turnover. This tabulation will be referred to in many future chapters as a tool to:

- rationalize the supplier mix to provide a smaller number of suppliers, giving the opportunity to increase the chosen suppliers' turnover, and permit the negotiation of improved prices and improved other benefits;
- to establish a base for economic forecasting;
- to provide the beginnings of an understanding of the work purchasing has to do;
- to assist in establishing departmental workload etc.

Question 2

The breakdown of costs to the level of works cost:

60% material costs
15% labour
25% overheads

With this information, you can see the scope there is for LUC (lowest ultimate cost) activities.

Material costs:	Are entirely your baby!
Labour costs:	You affect this indirectly if the labour are put on waiting time, or overtime, due to material shortages!
Overhead costs:	The answer to 1 showed 1130 suppliers of whom many will be contributing directly to overhead cost.

The list of minor suppliers will include:

Travel:	(Probably not a purchasing responsibility)
Stationery:	(Purchasing reponsibility)
Hotels and conferences:	(Probably Sales/Marketing)
Capital equipment:	(Normally handled by Facilities, Plant Engineering etc.)
Cars/trucks:	(Managing director?)
Buildings:	(Managing director?)
Building maintenance:	(Plant Engineering)

Canteen:	(Personnel?)
Safety equipment:	(Plant Engineering)
Prototype Engineering:	(Design Engineering)

Some of these purchases are made based on special budgets but, in all cases, Purchasing should control these purchases. The usual result of investigation shows every form of malpractice through ignorance and enormous waste, whenever the 'amateur buyers' are allowed to buy. This is regrettably true, even if the MD is the amateur buyer in question!

The above list of items could easily amount to £3 000 000 of the £4 000 000 spent on 'minor suppliers', with capital making the other £1 000 000.

Remembering the complaints of the boss, Purchasing will have to get hold of these purchases too.

The perceptive manager will recognize that he or she will be getting into a political hassle with the NIMBYs (not in my back yard), but it's a battle which will have to be fought and won!

Question 3

The answer to question 3 reveals that Accounting are experiencing a high percentage of consumable-type items where the invoice shows a different price to their order copy and a considerable number of invoices are received for goods where an order has never been issued!

There can be many reasons for this, chief among which will be the 'amateur buyers' who will telephone a supplier for delivery and ask for the goods to be delivered to them at their office location. So an order *never* is created! Instead, the amateur buyer obtains a cheque from Accounts.

Where an order exists but the price on the invoice is different, the most usual cause is that the current price has not been checked with the supplier before further supplies have been requested.

The suppliers and the requisitioners who are causing the highest number of these queries have been listed by Accounts; and Purchasing will have to deal with this problem soon. It must be remembered that while there are excellent opportunities for supplier rationalization and cost savings, you may well be on the brink of uncovering large-scale theft as you investigate this aspect. Sad to say, where Purchasing is not in the driving seat, some people will be 'on the fiddle' and in a high percentage of cases where Purchasing start to get a 'grip', they virtually fall over these crimes!

Question 4

Supplier payment is a very important area where cash flow control can be exerted. However, 'control' can be seriously mismanaged and the Purchasing Manager has to get a grip quickly on the following aspects.

Assuming that the Accounts department stated that they paid suppliers 30 days after the end of the month in which the goods were delivered, means that the average time the supplier has to wait for payment is 45 days.

- This payment period is in fact determined not by Accounting – but by Purchasing! It is part of the bargain when prices are negotiated.
- It is possible to negotiate with the majority of suppliers for any payment period from cash with order down to, say, 90 days after the goods have been received or, indeed, in certain cases, much longer periods.
- Suppliers have to borrow from the bank to fund longer payment periods and their price will reflect this – provided that at the time of placing the order, they were aware of the payment period. But they rely on being paid in line with the payment period to which the buyer has agreed.
- Accounting, however, often are given an instruction in order to protect 'cash flow' to look at the monthly balance sheet and to compare the cash received from customers against the cash due to suppliers, wages, VAT payments, utilities, debts etc. Since bank interest is high, the instruction to do this is driven by the need to reduce borrowing or prevent it entirely!

  When this instruction is issued, it also often demands that there is a positive cash flow position held at all times, so that even if the two sides of the equation balance, only say 70% of the cash owed can be paid and, in that instance, suppliers come last!
- Purchasing therefore in this scenario has been forced to take part in a con trick perpetrated on the suppliers. Accounting will then ask Purchasing to decide which suppliers should be paid on this month's cheque run. (This is a real judgement call!)
- Naturally, the suppliers who don't get paid feel they have been robbed. They react by supplying customers who do pay on time first and if there is any spare capacity, they will supply you. Then, if the situation continues, they put you on 'stop' where they refuse to deliver until their payments are brought up to date.
- This spiral of problems escalates as the suppliers chosen to replace the ones who had put you on 'stop' also find they can't get paid and so they too put you on 'stop'.

- Eventually, the only way you can obtain materials is by paying cash on delivery – and where's cash flow then?

If Purchasing are able to get hold of this problem quickly, it is possible to negotiate, at least with the top suppliers, let us say 120 days' payment delay and this provides a cash flow holiday. Often, Accounting do not tell Purchasing what they're doing until it's too late. This is an aspect that requires eternal vigilance!

Questions 5 and 6

Quality control have now provided you with a list of the components and materials supplied, and the suppliers who supply them, where high reject rates are experienced.

This is the foundation for a quality improvement programme and the way this is linked to a major cost reduction drive will be referred to in detail in later chapters.

This list should be compared with the categories of inspection from 100% piece inspection through to supplier assurance.

Clearly, if all your suppliers could be upgraded to Supplier Assurance grade, there are considerable cost savings to be made.

The reasons for this are as follows.

- If a large number of suppliers who deliver material which The Company has to inspect can transfer to supplier assurance grades, this frees up inspectors for re-deployment.
- Cost savings result if the suppliers assure their own quality; since rejects returned by The Company incur transport costs, rework or scrap, and the total cost of the batch has to be borne by the suppliers. They should be able to reduce their prices because their costs have been reduced.
- More and more companies are driving to become quality assured, either via BS5750 routines, or by the quality assurance (Q101) programmes initiated by Ford, or other similar processes employed by other major companies. If their supplier's suppliers are quality assured, this makes the supplier more attractive to do business with than one who has not.
- If suppliers do not improve their quality fast, then the answer is to resource. You cannot afford to pay for other people's inefficiencies!

Question 7

Manufacturing/Assembly have given you the list of the major offenders by part number, description, supplier and the number of times that failure to meet delivery dates have caused shortages and delays in production.

Again, this is an area of great importance and some very thorough analysis work is required.

- Which of the items which were late were long-lead items?
- Which were the result of being called up too late?
- Which were the result of late rejections?
- Which were just late? (Clearly somebody's finger trouble!)

You will be able to establish cause for each of these categories and prepare a hit list as part of a supply improvement programme.

Question 8

Production Control had already stated that Sales/Marketing promises to customers were often very tight. By investigating the lead times allowed by Production Control, a strong correlation will be found between late call-off from Production Control and suppliers being unable to meet the required delivery date.

Lead-time problems

These can be solved in a variety of ways. This is another matter which will recur many times throughout this book, but suffice to say that ways to solve the problem include these.

- Investigation as to why the supplier wants a lead time of four months. Perhaps they do not order raw material until they get your order and raw material is on three months' delivery or perhaps they have their own shop-sequencing problems etc. You may well be able to persuade the supplier to hold raw materials or finished stock on a bond stock basis – or a consignment stock – or you may be able to find a supplier with faster reaction times.
- Perhaps Sales/Marketing could provide a forecast which they had confidence to allow you to order against, perhaps giving a year's horizon on which to plan deliveries.

There are many other methods available which will be discussed later on in the book.

Late rejects

This area will be covered by the quality improvement programme that you will set up.

The last category that Manufacturing reported was 'just late'. Quite often, Production Control and Purchasing are guilty, either jointly or severally.

Examples include:

- wrong stock figures which have misled Production Control into believing that stock existed and a 'panic' to get more was dropped into Purchasing's lap at the last minute;
- a late engineering change was implemented and a decision was taken to incorporate the change too soon;
- sheer finger trouble in Purchasing where material was not expedited in time or at all;
- supplier strikes, factory fires, lorry crashes etc.

Ninety-nine per cent of the causes of shortages of all types can be eliminated.

Shortage lists are the bane of every Purchasing department's life and no excuse/reason is ever accepted sympathetically.

The writer, on one memorable occasion, had three items on the shortage list to answer for:

- a small ship carrying steel had sunk;
- a factory due to deliver that day had burned down the previous night;
- material due to be flown in from India that day had been eaten the day before by a tiger!

The deadpan reception was, 'OK, but when do we get some more?'

Even these shortages need not have occurred if more forethought had been given and, in the ensuing chapters, supply protection will be referred to in many different ways.

Questions 9 and 10

These deal with mark-up percentages and profit contribution. The way in which Purchasing contains the works cost input into materials varies depending on the type of manufacturer.

If the environment is a mass-produced environment – let us say cars, a reduction of a few coppers on a casting may save many hundreds of thousands of pounds per annum – but passes into profit – rather than on to the customer, since car prices are not sensitive to a saving of 10p on all gear boxes.

On the other hand, a carelessly conceded price increase on a casting for a one-off product may directly impact on profit, plus necessitating a price increase being generated to the customer.

FORGING A LINK WITH FINANCE AND MARKETING

In the extremes from mass production to a one-off product and everything which lies between, a very comprehensive system must be set up which links to Finance and Marketing that:

- reports current prices versus standard costs;
- reports on savings and losses against current prices certainly, and possibly also against standard costs;
- reports on the forecast of expected price movement for the next 12 months;
- provides a savings plan to offset forecast price increases;
- from time to time targets certain products for special cost reduction exercises.

THE FIRST SEVEN ACTION PLANS

It will be seen that the answers to the 10 questions have provided the basis for:

- a cost reduction programme;
- a supply improvement programme;
- a quality improvement programme;
- a linkage from Purchasing to Marketing and Finance on price movement, current and forecast;
- a supplier reduction programme;
- a detailed examination of the depredations of the 'amateur buyers';
- an action plan to attack lead-time problems.

These seven programmes will answer all but two of the MD's initial directives. The two remaining are contracts and capital purchases. These will be dealt with in later chapters.

2

PEOPLE AND MONEY

The first seven action programmes identified in Chapter 1 are the tip of the iceberg in running a purchasing department, so staffing is necessary to run the routine operations before trying to meet the MD's objectives.

SOLVING THE STAFFING EQUATION

The staffing equation is dependent on two factors: list of operations and time required; and the working time available.

List of operations and time required

This means how much time is spent in the buying process, which includes:

1. discussions with designers in the case of new releases;
2. discussions with Production Control, Manufacturing, Quality Control, Accounting etc.;
3. discussions with potential suppliers;
4. raising enquiries;
5. evaluating quotations and preparation of quotation analysis;
6. source choice, final negotiation, writing up record and history card;
7. raising the order, circulating accounts and production control with the order copies;
8. progressing samples;
9. progressing regular requirements;
10. special exercises.

The working hours available

The normal working week is 37.5 hours excluding overtime paid at premium rates – say a total of 40 hours per week. There are normally four weeks' annual leave allowed and, depending on the company policy, another week to two weeks of other holidays.

So we have 40 hours × 46 weeks, i.e. 1840 hours. Deduct personal time, so say, 1700 hours per annum are the hours per head available.

The list of operations that the buyer has to carry out has been expressed above as though the whole task is carried out with the buyer keeping manually maintained buying records, the enquiries and orders being typed, the quotation analysis being written up manually, order circulation being carried out through the internal mail, records showing total turnover by supplier being kept manually, names and addresses maintained by filing clerks, all copy documents filed centrally – and so on.

The true buying activities in the list of operations are all those which exclude a paperworking element. So the type of system that the buyers will be equipped with is a very important factor in headcount.

The list of processes do not have to be completed in all cases in all buying operations.

For example, if it is a reorder on an existing supplier, the buyer may normally have to complete just (6), (7) and (9). On the other hand, a major casting could take up many hours of discussions and negotiations. The system must be able to cope with both extremes.

Many very effective labour-saving negotiations can be achieved, for example, if all prices with a supplier are agreed for a year and the buyer does not have to negotiate the items on this order for subsequent requirements. So reordering is reduced to a minimum in time spent. However, all new items released for the first time have to undergo all the processes listed, whether manual or computerized systems are in use.

Normally, the more expensive the item, the longer the processes take, although a simple bolt which is required to be made to special requirements can take as long as the most difficult casting to source.

ESTABLISHING THE WORKLOAD

On the study provided by Finance/Accounting, giving the suppliers in descending order of turnover, it may be that they can possibly also tell you how many part numbers/items were employed – giving you a fair feeling for the number of components brought in during the year. It may be to feed a mass-production unit where deliveries are required weekly, for example, or a batch producing unit where the materials are brought in, say, four times per annum, or they could all be one-offs.

On production items, you can quickly arrive at an intake rate which may, as a broad average, produce a picture like this:

Castings	100 different types weekly
Pressings	500 different types weekly
Forgings	60 different types weekly
Rubber mouldings	40 different types weekly
Electrics/electronic	1500 different types weekly
Standard parts	300 different types weekly
Steel	80 different types weekly etc.

Discussion with Production Control and Engineering will give you an indication of the number of *new* items released monthly. This may present a picture like this:

Castings	5 per month
Pressings	20 per month
Forgings	5 per month
Rubber mouldings	10 per month
Electrics/electronic	50 per month
Standard parts	15 per month
Steel	3 per month etc.

The non-production load is best analysed by taking say a month's requisitions of which Accounting should hold copies and here you may find something in the order of 50 per day – all asking for delivery within a week!

If you have buyers on the staff who have some experience of buying within the systems you have available, then they should be able to give you an indication of the time it takes to carry out the procedures necessary across the range of items Purchasing are responsible for. From the information that you obtain you should be able to prepare a chart such as that shown in Table 2.1.

You must get the best advice you can at this point because although you can make adjustments up or down in headcount later, it is best to be as accurate as you can right from the 'off'.

Table 2.1 Assessment of working hours required

Commodity	First release	Number PA	Total hours	Re-order	Number PA	Total hours	Total hours per commodity	Annual spend per commodity	Number of suppliers
Castings	10 hours	60	600	0.30	5 000	2 500	3 100	£2m	10
Pressings	3 hours	240	720	0.30	25 000	12 500	13 220	£3m	5
Electrics/ Electronics	2 hours	600	1 200	0.05	75 000	6 250	7 450	£7m	19
Utilities	–	–	–	3.00	3	9	9	£1m	3
Rubber mouldings	3 hours	120	360	0.50	2 000	1 667	2 027	£1m	3
Forgings	5 hours	60	300	0.40	60	40	340	£1m	6
Standard parts	1 hour	180	180	0.10	15 000	2 500	2 680	£2m	11
Paint	2 hours	4	8	0.10	150	25	33	£1m	4
Copper	1 hour	100	100	0.30	200	100	200	£1m	3
Steel	3 hours	36	108	1.00	4 000	4 000	4 108	£2m	6
Consumables	1 hour	400	400	0.10	20 000	3 333	3 733	£3m (est)	1 070
			3 976			29 324	36 900	£24m	1 140

+ CAPITAL SOURCES 60

EXPENDITURE £1m

ASSESSMENT OF WORKING HOURS REQUIRED

Table 2.1 only accounts for £24 million of the £25 million which has been identified. The remaining million will be almost certainly capital equipment and, for the moment, this is set aside to avoid complication.

In Table 2.1 it is assumed that each repeated requirement has to go through a fresh order issue. It also assumes in the cases of electrics/electronics, standard parts and consumables that several parts are ordered from the supplier on the same order.

If The Company is able to issue monthly schedules to all production suppliers, then the reordering process is eliminated. Instead, an order for all items can be established with all components listed and prices agreed for, say, a year. Volumes do not have to be shown on the order since the instrument of the order is the schedule. In this case, the reordering content can be replaced with an expediting function.

CHOICE OF STRUCTURE

There are many advantages to the blanket order/scheduling process, which relieves the buyer of bashing out thousands of orders per annum, responding to Production Control's latest released requirement.

First, an expeditor can maintain progress with a considerable number of components, and ensure delivery by obtaining promises from the suppliers and keeping them to their promises from the expeditor's copy of the schedule sent to the supplier.

Secondly, expeditors can be trained in a matter of two to three months to be effective and, after further training and study, form the best source for up and coming buyers.

Salaries for expeditors are lower than those of buyers and suitable personnel are more easily found.

Thirdly, because they are progressing a defined number of suppliers and components, they quickly become able to scent a problem and refer it upwards in good time for senior personnel to become involved; and they are the 'mass of manoeuvre' for travelling to suppliers, running around the factory to check stock, go to supply meetings etc.

An expeditor's job is attractive to young people of A level standard who want to make Purchasing their career and are willing to study for professional qualifications. Normally, on a weekly delivery basis, a single expeditor should be able to carry 600 to 700 items and up to 30 to 40 suppliers.

An item count should be carried out – assuming that there were, say, 4000 items in regular use, 7 expeditors would be well able to take care of all the reordering hours.

If the company is equipped with a system which depends on a new order for each call-off then, apart from any typing back-up, the 36 900 hours would require 22 buyers and support staff.

If it were possible to use expeditors, then the negotiation element would require 3976 hours, say 3 buyers and 7 expeditors. Possibly for coverage purposes, it would be advisable to add 3 junior buyers as assistants to the 3 buyers – but the difference is still 13 staff with blanket ordering and scheduling versus 22 staff without.

If the systems are not up to the mark, it may be necessary to go for the bigger number and introduce systems which do allow blanket order/scheduling at some time in the future. The eventual aim should be a 'paperless office' where all documentation is electronically produced.

Proceeding on the assumption that the assessment of working hours reflects the work process, then Table 2.1 gives the clue to the departmental organization necessary.

Clearly, specialist sections will have to be formed and the four criteria are:

- allied technologies should, whenever possible, be grouped together and no technology should be spread across two sections;
- turnovers on the sections are desirably close to each other;
- staffing is appropriate to the workload;
- number of items should be compared to workload, i.e. if reordering a casting takes 30 minutes, and 6 electronic components can be reordered in 30 minutes, a good work balance has been achieved, at a component ratio of 1:6.

On examination of the assessment of working hours, those sections can be created as follows:

- pressings section with 13 200 hours would need a total staff of 8, which would be one section's work;
- by combining rubber mouldings with electrics/electronics, 9447 hours indicate a requirement for a total staff of 6;
- castings and forgings combined with standard parts, steel, paint and copper provide a total of 10 461 hours, equating to 6 staff;
- consumables are estimated as having 3733 hours of labour plus utilities which provides work for a staff of 2. It may be that when

Table 2.2 Proposed establishment of sections

Section	Total hours	New	Repeat	Heads: workload	Turnover
Pressings	13 220	720	12 500	8	£3m
Electronics/electrics and rubber mouldings	9 447	1 560	7 917	6	£8m
Castings/forgings/ standard parts/paint/ copper and steel	10 461	1 296	9 165	6	£9m
Consumables and utilities	3 733	400	3 333	2	£4m
Capital					£1m*
Staff total				22	

* When capital workload is established, one more head may be required.

the capital purchase is added to this section, a further head will need to be recruited.

PROPOSED ESTABLISHMENT OF SECTIONS

It is possible that one or two secretaries will also be required to deal with typing, filing, booking travel etc. and, excluding yourself, this makes the department 25 strong.

Making the ratio of turnover to heads £1 million per head. This is not an exceptional ratio, either too great or too little – but we have already seen that it can be improved drastically if new systems can be implemented. However, bearing in mind the improvement programmes and the savings possibilities that have to be implemented, this is not the time to be too worried about ratios.

STAFFING

Ideally, a better balance than the one that has emerged could have been achieved had it been possible to amalgamate consumables with the electronics section but, since the buying processes employed are quite different, it is wise to keep the consumables section separate, even although it is less than one-third the size of the others.

Because the three bigger sections are all geared directly to production while the consumables area is driven by requisitions for materials such as lavatory paper, lubricants, safety shoes, light bulbs, electrical fittings, plumber's requirements, stationery and so on, priorities are different.

This being the case, we are going to be looking at four senior buyers (or chief buyers) who are specialists in the commodity groups which form the backbone of the four sections.

The salary band of these high-grade professionals will be, at 1993 levels, in the range of £16 000 to £20 000 per annum.

Below the chief buyer grade an assortment of buyers, junior buyers and purchasing assistants will be required. Job descriptions for each of these grades and the purchasing manager will be found in Appendix A.

Pressing section

In order to establish the skills required, it is necessary to establish areas of responsibility within the section.

The chief buyer will be the top negotiator and trouble-shooter, and will take on the most sensitive buys. He or she will also be responsible for discipline and, most importantly of all, agreeing with you the policies you wish the pressing section to conform to and to ensure, and report their implementation.

Underneath the chief buyer, there is the business of the new 'buys' to handle, plus the very heavy reordering load. Clearly, too, there is a considerable amount of recording, keeping records up to date and so on.

Also, there is a certainty of a heavy load of tooling which has to be purchased for the new buys and, since the tooling is transferable, it may mean that each reordering necessitates a re-enquiry. If another source proves more competitive than the current holder, then the tooling and raw material has to be transferred.

WORKLOAD ALLOCATION WITHIN A SECTION

The allocation could be that Mr A (buyer) handles all deep-drawn pressings, both new buys and reorders. Miss B handles all guillotine presswork and reorders. Mrs C (buyer) handles all sheet metal work and reorders. Mr D (buyer) handles all fabrications plus reorders. It may well be that sheet steel (as distinct from the bar which is bought for the factory by another section) is free issued, in which case, Mr E (buyer) may have this as his responsibility.

Because of the huge amount of paperwork which has to be generated, the remaining two people are recruited as purchasing assistants to support the efforts of the others.

If the pressings chief buyer is recruited first, that individual will be able to decide exactly the allocation method.

Nevertheless, the section looks like requiring:

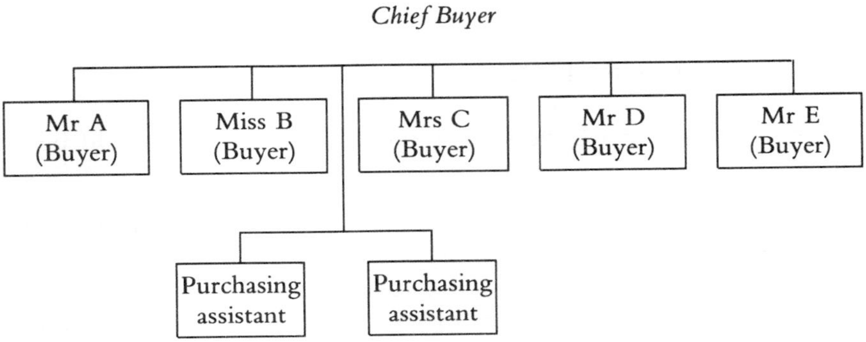

The electrics/electronics and rubber section

This section would be headed by a chief buyer who is a specialist in the electrical and electronic field, but would have the same role as the pressings chief buyer. The team of five would be deployed as follows:

- one electronics buyer;
- two electrics buyers;
- one rubber buyer;
- one purchasing assistant.

It might well be that the electrics buyer might, in order to get the work balance right, have to carry some electronics as well.

The castings, forgings, standard parts and raw materials section

This section would also be headed by a chief buyer with the same organizational role as his or her colleagues, but who is a specialist in castings and forgings. The team would be:

- one castings buyer;
- one standard parts buyer;

- one forgings and raw materials buyer;
- two purchasing assistants.

Consumables section

As a simple consumables section, a highly experienced buyer would be adequate – but capital is a significant buy, so the chief buyer appointed to run the section should be a capital equipment buyer and, as this work grows, an extra purchase assistant will be required, making the section three strong.

RECRUITING (Salaries at 1993 levels)

Assuming four chief buyers are required, salary levels could be as follows.

(a) Salary £16 000 to £20 000 per annum. Each chief buyer has to have good experience in the speciality areas required.
(b) Thirteen buyers with good experience each in some of the various commodity responsibilities identified. Salary £14 000 to £16 000 per annum.
(c) Purchasing assistants – six required. Salary £9000 to £11 000 per annum. (One is not required immediately.)

Assuming all staff are recruited at the lower end of the starting salaries, the salary bill would be:

		£
Chief buyers	4 at £16 000	64 000
Buyers	13 at £14 000	182 000
Purchasing assistants	6 at £ 9000	54 000
Total		£300 000

=1.2% of department turnover
(Excluding pension contributions, NHI etc.)

If your purchasing team can get their teeth into the profit improvement programmes identified in Chapter 1, net savings of 5% plus of departmental turnover can be easily achieved full year. We all have to speculate to accumulate – even your boss! So the boss's money has to be put where his or her mouth is! The savings potential is at least £1.2 million.

Depending on your locality, it may be possible to advertise locally for your junior staff – but your chief buyers and the specialist buyers will most probably prove to be national appointments.

In this case, the chief buyer and buyer appointments should be advertised in the *Daily Telegraph* and the *Institute of Purchasing* magazine.

THE TYPICAL BUYER PROFILE

For someone who is new to purchasing management, recruiting is quite daunting even if The Company Personnel Manager is a reliable supporter. It is perhaps worthwhile to give you a thumbnail sketch of a typical buyer's career path.

Most start in junior positions in purchasing such as expeditors, purchasing assistants, junior buyers, or they may come into purchasing from engineering, accounting, banking or other disciplines.

Nearly all have good A levels, or banking, accounting or similar basic qualifications such as Ordinary National Certificate (ONC) or Higher National Certificate (HNC), and a fair percentage start off as graduates.

As they progress through the various commodity areas, many study and pass their Chartered Institute of Purchasing examinations. (The Institute of Purchasing and Supply received its Royal Charter in mid-1992.) This exam is rated above HNC and requires the student to pass the following subjects:

Foundation Stage
Economics
English business law
Business accounting
Management principles and administration
Introduction to purchasing and materials management

Professional Stage (Compulsory subjects)
Purchasing and supply management I
Policy and organization
Purchasing and supply management II
Practice and techniques
Purchasing and supply management III
Logistics and distribution
Purchasing and supply management IV
Legal applications
Research study

Case study

Professional Stage (Elective subjects)
Materials and production management
Marketing
Project and contracts management
Purchasing and supply in the public sector
Retail merchandise management
International purchasing

The course of study is very often carried out over three to four years of evening classes, although there are some students who gain their diploma with full-time study.

Thus, the buyer is unlikely to be less than the age of 24 before obtaining a diploma and possibly has up to four years' purchasing experience in buying.

If the buyer's experience has been with companies allied to your own, he or she should be suitable for employment with you.

The buyer should be able to show that he or she has participated in some of the seven special programmes and should have the confidence to run his or her responsibility with confidence, and he should also be able to discuss his or her best pieces of work.

As career development continues, the buyer will have been given more responsibility and perhaps some staff, and will probably be a senior buyer in his or her own company. Senior buyer is a 'rating' rather than a rank.

At this time, the buyer will be looking for a Chief Buyer position and if that is not forthcoming in his or her own company, the buyer will be sampling the employment market. This age group are usually 28 to 35 years old.

All things being equal, the buyer will be suitable as one of your section heads (chief buyers).

It may well be that you will spot young buyers who are too green, or not fully qualified, but exhibit very good potential. It is possible to recruit them at a junior buyer grade on a lower salary scale with the intention of developing them along the lines of the 'typical buyer profile', salary range £11 000 to £12 000.

Purchasing Assistants

Unless there are people capable of transferring from within your own company, then these too are recruited from outside, but locally advertised.

Ideally, they should have their A levels and be interested in a career in Purchasing, they should be reasonably numerate and methodical people, but with some imaginative flair.

Ideally, they should be aged 18 to 20. Starting salary will be around £9000 to £11 000. You may find it strategically important, however, to bring in some much older people to give stability to a department which will have quite a young team.

The job descriptions in Appendix A present the 'scope' that your new recruits should be able to deploy as soon as they are in place.

If you are unable to recruit all the buyers precisely, with the different specialities which are desirable, do not despair. A well-trained buyer in one branch of engineering can be operational in another within two weeks and earning their corn in three months. Companies in defence, auto industry, aviation, electric and electronic have close parallels to each other, and buyers in these areas are accustomed to have to take a new commodity range, and having a complete grip inside a few days. Some well-respected buyers in the pharmaceutical industry started their buying careers in engineering.

The balance of purchasing assistants to buyers varies according to the amount of paperwork and volume of components passing through the sections.

The consumables section at this stage does not have a purchasing assistant. It is probable that the buyer would be able to fill this role because complexity of work, with the exception of capital, is not so high as in the other sections. But capital is a 'slow build-up' job and will take some time to become significant.

This situation must be kept under review as a purchasing assistant will eventually be required.

THE HIERARCHICAL STRUCTURE

There are many ways of organizing the structure of a Purchasing department – but the hierarchical structure never changes. There are many reasons for this which will become clearer as the reader continues reading this book. As an example, it could well be reasonable to amalgamate all the purchase assistants and form a section headed by one of the purchase assistants, reporting to the purchasing manager, acting as a service to all four sections.

There are many questions then which arise.

(a) Has the manager the time to devote?
(b) Does the manager want to deprive his or her sections of resources?

(c) Will the PA section lose its sense of priorities if not in direct contact with the buying group?

The job descriptions contained in Appendix A are a distillation of the observations taken over many hundreds of companies and are very commonly used in industry, where expediting as a separate function has been created or the type of 'buy' precludes the use of expeditors. In any event, all buying staff must be prepared to progress materials as appropriate.

Detailed job descriptions for the posts of purchasing manager, chief buyer, buyer and purchasing assistant can be found in Appendix A.

3

MATERIALS

Chapter 2 described the 'Personnel' and the 'Money' aspects of staffing a purchasing department. In order to have a functioning department, there are a range of materials that are required. The first material to be considered is – where will the department sit?

OFFICE LAYOUT

The office accommodation may be open plan; or offices for yourself and each of the chief buyers with the buyers seated in section offices (closed offices), or anything in between.

There are some essentials to consider.

First, with regard to the British Standards minimum for working space, lighting and heating; your own facilities department can advise you, but in the writer's opinion, the BS standard for working space allocation is cramped, the lighting standard is only just acceptable and the heating standard is lower than most people prefer, so good managers should try to ensure that their department has the right level of physical comfort by using personal judgement, beyond satisfying the legal minimum. Natural light and local control of environment are also desirable.

Secondly, the seating plan has some other quite subtle considerations to be addressed. It is always advisable to lay out an office plan which pays attention to the hierarchy in the department – this is helpful in supporting working disciplines. For example, if one of the chief buyers has to speak to the purchasing manager, it is not acceptable if the chief buyer just shouts across the office to the purchasing manager. It is much better if the chief buyer has to leave his or her own desk and walk to the purchasing manager to see the boss in the boss's office or space.

The same applies with the relationship between the buyers and their chief buyer.

If the purchasing office has these unspoken hierarchical divisions, discipline is expressed without underlining rank differences.

Further, there is the aspect of synergy to consider. Considering the buying section responsible to a given chief buyer, there are always some of the team away from the desk. They may be visiting suppliers, at meetings, or running around the factory; aside from annual vacations. It is important that every telephone caller gets a rapid response from purchasing, so, if a telephone rings at an empty desk, someone must answer it! They should then solve the caller's problem if it's urgent or take a message.

Equally, because the buyers are at different levels of development, they hear and learn from the way others deal with situations, so it is very useful for raising the level of the individual skills if buyers are within earshot of each other.

Where this synergistic advantage is recognized and required, it is usual to seat buyers together. So if a 'closed office' structure is used, two or three buyers per office meets this requirement; or if 'open plan', the buyers' desks can be placed together, either in pairs, or as a complete block where all the desks are together, by section.

Buyers, chief buyers and the purchasing manager need space for meetings and space for visitors.

Many of these meetings are face-to-face meetings between the buyer and a representative, and it is useful if there is space by the buyer's desk, and a visitor's chair, where these meetings can take place.

Some meetings will require a considerable attendance and thus, since these are regular occurrences, purchasing additionally needs its own conference room.

It is usual for visitors to be offered coffee or tea and since it is an incredible waste of time to have secretaries constantly brewing up, it is advisable to have a machine where coffee and tea can be provided on demand.

Telephones, fax machines etc. are essential to allow fast and effective communication. In a normal purchasing department, the essential calls that have to be made contribute to more than 50% of the company's telephone bill.

Thus, apart from internal telephone calls which are also very heavily used by purchasing, it seems unavoidable that each person has his or her own instrument. Depending on the amount of reliance to be placed on computer systems, VDUs can be shared between two or provided on a one-each basis.

LOCATION OF THE PURCHASING DEPARTMENT

The location of the purchasing office is also a very important consideration. The four departments with whom purchasing must be in very close contact are:

- Production;
- Production Control;
- Design Engineering;
- Facilities Engineering.

If any of these departments are separated by an open space, such as a loading bay, and the buyers and the members of the four departments have to cross that open space to visit each other, it will be as though that space is a gulf thousands of miles wide and each department will tend to work in isolation, 'doing its own thing'.

Synergy between these departments is vital so it is very important that, wherever possible, the departments are located side by side. If this cannot be achieved, Purchasing will have to 'bridge' the gulf and this is difficult.

DEPARTMENTAL IMAGE

Probably, there is a decor and furnishings company policy in existence, and the Purchasing department will be no exception in conforming to this. However, the Purchasing department represents the company to the public and the impression that it gives to visitors is important.

If the company policy dictated 'deluxe' type furniture, the impression visiting representatives would gain would be that the company had plenty of money and could afford to be generous in the prices they pay.

Equally, if the offices of the Purchasing department are a shambles, the company's reputation is adversely affected – because word gets around very quickly in the market.

This leaves you with the choice of image that you, as manager, want to project to suit your own 'management style'.

The writer's preference is to project an image of good functional equipment and furniture, with an atmosphere of busy, controlled activity.

THE FIRST PROCEDURE

In order to control the operations of the department, the manager has to be able to issue instructions and to explain the policy behind the instructions given. Further details are addressed in Chapter 6 but an important area which must be 'procedurized' from the beginning is that of the processes associated with what is often called 'quote and select' and demonstrates the requirement for another type of material – paper!

Whether your 'system' is a fully computerized one or a manual system, the following procedure *has* to be put in place and must reflect the company policy.

A request to purchase any form of customer requirement arrives within the purchasing department. This can vary from a new engineering release to a piece of capital equipment.

The buying card

The first step after recording receipt of the release, or requisition, and the initiator, lies in the buyer's record – which may be held on the VDU or a simple buying card on a cardex system, and is prepared by the buyer.

The essential information will be:

part number;
description;
quantity required;
date of requirement of samples;
production date required;
engineering design level;
initiator; and
date received in department.

(In some systems, this information is transferred via the VDU system from design engineering and this detail forms the buying card automatically.)

The next duty of the buyer is to examine the drawings, specifications and any other detail provided, and prepare an enquiry list. The minimum number of potential suppliers should very rarely be less than three and up to six is reasonable.

The enquiry

This is, at its simplest, a market study to see who 'out there' can provide your requirement at the lowest ultimate cost.

The judgement basis has to be:

- quality;
- quantity;
- time; and
- price.

The enquiry to all potential suppliers must contain exactly the same information in terms of what is required. It must also provide the potential supplier with the Terms and Conditions under which the company trades. For example, the Terms and Conditions may contain a requirement for payment by The Company in 60 days. Some potential suppliers would 'regret' the enquiry on those grounds alone, as they only want to trade at 30 days.

As suppliers return their quotations, an analysis should be prepared which allows in-depth comparison to take place.

The quotation analysis

It will be seen from the sample quotation analysis shown here that several solutions might have been chosen if the quotation analysis method of logging the incoming quotations is not employed. The quotations are only expressed in the same comparable terms if the enquiry is clear and asks for identical information.

A buyer in a hurry might have selected Romeo since they could get off the ground fastest – but the combination of tool cost and high unit price made them the dearest and they would not accept 60-day payment.

A buyer looking at unit price would probably have accepted Foxtrot because their unit price was lowest and they could get very close to the lead time required. But, in fact, analysis shows they would have been the most expensive and would only accept 45-day payment!

Between the two remaining, Tango and Delta, it is really a no-brain decision, Delta's quality is better than Tango's and the three-year cost is cheaper by going to Delta.

Having selected Delta, this should not stop the buyer going back to them and asking for a reduction in either unit price or tool cost, or both, without of course telling the supplier that they are already the lowest quote, in order to ensure that they have achieved the lowest ultimate cost.

QUOTATION ANALYSIS

PART NUMBER	304–6150	QUANTITY REQUIRED	1000/month
DESCRIPTION	Bolt (special)	DATE OF REQUIREMENT	6 weeks from order
PAYMENT TERMS	60 days		

SUPPLIER	PRICE (EACH)	DELIVERY	TOOL COST	PAYMENT TERMS	PAST QUALITY	PAST SUPPLY
TANGO LIMITED	30p	6 weeks	£ 2 000	Accept 60	Very good	Good
ROMEO LIMITED	45p	5 weeks	£ 700	30 days	Average	Good
DELTA LIMITED	30p	6 weeks	£ 900	Accept 60	Excellent	Good
FOXTROT LIMITED	25p	6/7 weeks	£ 4 000	45 days max	Average	Good
ANALYSIS	MODEL LIFE	VOLUME × MODEL LIFE	VOL × UNIT PRICE	TOOL COST		
TANGO LIMITED	3 years	36 000	£10 800	£2 000	£12 800	
ROMEO LIMITED	3 years	36 000	£16 200	£ 700	£16 900	
DELTA LIMITED	3 years	36 000	£10 800	£ 900	£11 700	
FOXTROT LIMITED	3 years	36 000	£ 9 000	£4 000	£13 000	

Buyer Recommendation: DELTA LIMITED

The approval process

Having completed the quotation analysis – which can also be carried out on certain computer systems automatically, there needs to be an approval of recommendation step imposed.

The three-year value of this order would be £11 700 which, on a departmental turnover of £25 000 000, is a very small sum – but should a buyer who may be earning less than this sum be allowed the right to place orders like this without approval for the buyer's action? At what level must the buyer's decision be checked?

The buyer might not know that the chief buyer is carrying out, say, a cost-reduction exercise which, if successful, would provide a 20% reduction in all materials purchased from Tango and an improvement in quality standards – so the chief buyer should certainly have a sight of the buyer's actions.

From another point of view, the company's material supply position is being decided by a junior member of the organization and this perhaps needs verification by a senior.

There is also the question of buyer probity – most buyers never think of using the sums they disburse for any form of personal gain – the odd rogues do – and sometimes buyers are accused of 'fiddling', even if by chance they pick a bad supplier.

In order to avoid any of the above, it is prudent to have an approval system in place.

Clearly, all levels of Purchasing personnel will be carrying out negotiations and raising orders. If the chief buyer places an order, the purchasing manager should approve it; if the purchasing manager places an order, his or her boss should approve it, so each level is giving their senior an opportunity to cross-check their work.

The saviour in all this is that normally the purchasing manager would only be placing orders of the highest value, the chief buyers a lesser value and the buyers a lesser value still – but nothing is ever perfect.

If the bolt 304–6150 had been £3 each, the order value would have been £108 900 including tool cost, but the specialist bolt buyer would still have gone through the processes described and arrived at a recommendation. Thus, a junior buyer can be handling very expensive orders.

In order to meet this eventuality, the signature of the order level is defined. A typical signature level table looks like this:

Value of order	
£500–£10 000	No authorizing signature except buyer required.
£10 000–£50 000	Chief buyer approval mandatory.
£50 000–£1 000 000	Purchasing manager approval mandatory.
£1 000 000 and above	MD approval mandatory.

The order

If the 'approver' agreed the quotation analysis (and an example has been given as to why not), the order is then produced, signed by the buyer concerned (after verification) and countersigned by the approver.

(It is a point worth mentioning that in some computer systems, the quotation analysis is constructed on the buyer's VDU with the selected source underlined by the buyer on the screen; the buyer then transmits the quotation analysis on to the approver's screen. If the approver agrees, then he or she presses PRINT and the order is produced by the system.)

All that then remains is for the buyer to sign the order and dispatch it.

An example will be found at the end of this chapter.

The buying card again

The buying card is then brought up to date. All quotations received are logged with the date of the quotes, the successful supplier and order number are also noted.

If a computer system is used, the information should be 'filed' in four ways:

1. part number and supplier in part number order with latest prices;
2. suppliers in alphabetical order with latest price and date of order;
3. price history by supplier and by part number and order;
4. annual turnover by supplier.

If no computer support exists, the cross-referring process for items 1, 2 and 3 can be achieved by filing the buying cards in part number order by supplier, and the statistics (which *will* be required) handled by special exercises on an 'as and when' basis; it is a very time-consuming process, but the information provided from the four analyses is vital in negotiation and in other situations which emerge.

Terms and conditions

Before the first enquiry is raised or the first order placed, you have to establish under what conditions your company trades. So to have a good set of terms and conditions is a vital basic material, and this information should always appear on both enquiries and orders. No terms and conditions can be entirely all-embracing and special clauses are required to reflect requirements/agreements which either modify or override the terms and conditions. These are often referred to as 'front-of-order' conditions.

An example could be 'These items must be supplied in export-freight cases containing 12 per case'. But this is not to do with terms of trade and, consequently, it is added only when this condition is required.

Returning to the Delta bolt, our order would show on the front:

- the company name and address and buyer's name;
- the supplier's name and address;
- the part number and description of the item and unit price;
- the quantity required and any supply detail such as packing;
- schedule information, duration of order etc.;
- tool cost;
- date by which samples are required;
- date by which first delivery of bulk must be made;
- special conditions.

While the standard terms and conditions printed on the enquiry and the order (amounting to around 25 points) are very seldom varied, the special 'front of order' conditions are infinitely variable.

STANDARD TERMS AND CONDITIONS

1. Terms of payment

For example, 60 days from receipt of invoice etc. (or similar).

2. Force majeure

Actions to be undertaken by both parties in the event of *force majeure* (e.g. if they suffer a disaster which prevents them delivering or if the company suffers a problem which prevents the company taking the goods if presented on time). The buyer will endeavour to obtain a delay to give the supplier more time, but retains the right to buy from elsewhere if the supplier cannot deliver; and asks the supplier's help in not insisting on delivery and consequent payment until the company is able to accept delivery.

3. Quality

(a) Reject materials detected on receipt will be returned at supplier's cost.
(b) All items supplied must conform to the drawing specifications and other materials supplied.
(c) We reserve the right to rework rejected material at your cost and bill you if the need is urgent.

4. Samples off production tools

All samples submitted should be off production tools.

5. Confidentiality

Confidentiality must be maintained between the supplier and the company, and the supplier must not divulge to any third party any detail of company products they manufacture on the company's behalf.

6. Intellectual property

This remains the company's in all cases.

7. Packaging

No packaging supplied shall be returned. All packaging must be non-returnable.

8. Quotations

Quotations must include all packaging and delivery costs, and shall be presented as components of unit cost.

9. VAT

VAT must either be included in unit price or shown separately – the accountants will tell you what they want here.

10. Tooling payment

The supplier must indicate on the quotation tool cost and state whether the tool cost is full or part cost, and indicate in the latter case the percentage required by the supplier. (Capital equipment is not paid for by the company – only special tooling, jigs, fixtures etc.)

11. Price variation

Price cannot be varied except by submission to Purchasing (one month before the date the new price is required to take effect) of a properly constructed justification which Purchasing reserve the right to vary, dispute or reject, depending on circumstances.

Shorter intervals than one year between price increase requests are not normally approved.

12. Letting the order

The terms and conditions of this order are the only ones on which the order is awarded.

13. Quantity variation

Quantities on the order will not be varied, except by agreement by both parties.

14. Product liability

The supplier shall be responsible for compensating the company for consequential losses in the event of material failing in service. Suppliers are advised to indemnify themselves in case of this eventuality.

15. Sub-contract not generally permitted

Work awarded to the supplier shall not be sub-contracted unless approval is obtained prior to the action being taken being agreed by purchasing.

16. Flexible deliveries

The supplier is to endeavour at all times to be capable of responding to unscheduled requests and provide their best endeavours to meet these changed requirements.

17. Invoices

Suppliers are to submit invoices quoting part numbers, quantities and order number, with each delivery and at the end of each month, they should present a monthly statement to the Accounts department.

18. Invoice discrepancies

If invoices are presented which vary from the price on the order, the invoices will not be paid.

19. Purchase order amendments

Where an order price is varied, goods must not be invoiced at the new price until the supplier has received a purchase order amendment showing the revised price.

20. Time is of the essence

Delivery (where the supplier has been notified of a requirement, either by scheduled information or by dates shown on this order) time is considered to be of the essence of the order and failure to meet these dates may well result in cancellation of the order.

Consequential losses may well be claimed if these are incurred by the company as a result of failure to achieve delivery dates.

21. Materials bought in from extra territorial locations

All goods are to be delivered our works (DDP), unless otherwise instructed. In all cases, INCOTERMS must be employed.

22. Suppliers' responsibility for company tools and materials at their works

All tooling laid down by the company and drawings provided by the company shall be maintained in good order and should be adequately insured against all risks until the buyer informs the supplier in writing that the materials are no longer required and the supplier may dispose of them.

23. Applicable law

The applicable law is English law.

In the event of dispute between buyer and seller, arbitration can be applied by mutually agreed arbitrators.

The foregoing terms and conditions are basic to most industries, but must reflect the precise requirements of your own company policy.

If you are in an industry such as defence, a further range of terms and conditions are required, but these are not included here.

Because company lawyers would have to fight legislation on the basis of the company's terms and conditions, they need to be involved in the phraseology to be employed as they must be able to take the widest possible interpretation in order to defend the company in the event of legal action. It may well be necessary to re-jig these terms and, if any or either of you wish to amend these terms to embrace wider aspects, such as wider cancellation rights, then a meeting must be held between the purchasing manager and the company lawyers to finalize the phraseology before printing takes place – on both enquiries and orders! An example of a completed set of terms and conditions may be found in Appendix A.

Construction of the terms and conditions is absolutely vital and must be one of your first jobs.

THE WAR OF THE ACKNOWLEDGEMENTS

It is a strange quirk of law that, having arrived at the point of placing the order and having published your terms and conditions on the enquiry before the supplier quoted, the order only constitutes an offer and it does not constitute an agreement until the supplier acknowledges acceptance of the order.

It is a wise precaution to have a tear-off slip on the order which the supplier merely has to sign and return to complete this stage of the transaction.

Probably, about 50% of suppliers will sign return slips. Of the remaining 50%, 30% ignore the slip, don't acknowledge receipt of the order – but get on with it. (Since silence implies consent, they have accepted your conditions!) The remaining 20% reply with a letter thanking The Company for the order, and enclosing their own terms and conditions of acceptance.

Examples of the clauses they use are set out below.

1. We do not consider time to be of the essence.
2. Material varies from batch to batch and the company does not accept rejections for colour shade differences or dimensional differences.
3. We require payment at 30 days from receipt of goods.
4. We reserve the right to change material without reference to the customer etc.

Their supplier's lawyers have prepared these 'weasel-words' in order to get their companies off the hook in all events, except murder with ten eye-witnesses present!

Clearly these are in direct conflict with the terms and conditions you require the suppliers to conform to and, therefore, the purchasing department write contesting these conditions.

The battle of the acknowledgements has just started!

Clause 12 of the draft terms and conditions states: 'The terms and conditions of this order are the only ones on which the order is awarded.' It may be that your lawyer may not agree your use of this phrase since it cannot be enforced.

Incidentally, this quirk in the law exists on the Continent too and a French purchasing manager of the writer's acquaintance for many years had as his equivalent to Clause 12 on the draft terms and conditions herewith the following: 'Any variation to the terms and conditions on this order will be deemed not to have been received.'

He was horrified when a legal judgement proved this clause was only bluff and had no force.

What is, so far, successful is a modified Clause 12 which states, 'before any variation to the terms and conditions herewith are accepted, the supplier must have the modifications required in writing and signed by a director of the company'. (Directors have been known to spend 30 years wondering whether to sign their own expense report.)

The ridiculous part of all this is that, in nearly all cases, the buyer and the seller, irrespective of the terms and conditions on which the order is finally placed, actually behave with good commercial sense since the supplier doesn't want to lose business and the buyer wants what the buyer has ordered. As the purchasing department establishes an approved list of suppliers, each supplier, as a condition of being an approved supplier, agrees to conform to the company's terms and conditions. In such a case, a policy decision by the purchasing manager to modify the odd clause to ease the working relationship may be in order, but this device should only be employed sparingly.

PRICE VARIATION AND THE PURCHASE ORDER AMENDMENT

In the set of paper materials, there is one other essential. This is the purchase order amendment (POA).

Clauses 11, 17, 18 and 19 all refer to various aspects of price changes to a ruling order. It is often a 'front of order' condition in that 'prices are fixed for a defined period which is agreed at the time of placing the order, between the buyer and the supplier'. However, the supplier may find a price increase must be requested or the buyer may have negotiated a reduction and, after negotiation, the amount and date of the effect of the change has to be recorded, and the change implemented.

Rather than go through the whole routine of raising the order, it is much more convenient to raise an amendment.

This can also be used to cover:

- a change to engineering level;
- a modification to quantity;
- a modification to price;
- a modification to delivery location etc.

The circulation is the same as the order.

Following will be found a sample enquiry, order and purchase order amendment.

ENQUIRY

TO: THE SUPPLIER   FROM: THE COMPANY

DATE: 4 August 1992   CONTACT: ______

TEL NO: ______

WOULD YOU PLEASE PROVIDE YOUR QUOTATION FOR THE ITEMS, MATERIALS, GOODS OR SERVICES LISTED BELOW.

304–6150 Special Bolt 12 000 per annum
To be delivered in 1000 monthly lots
Samples required (6)
Sample delivery not later than 1 October 1992
First production delivery not later than 1 December 1992
* Drawings and specification enclosed
  Eng level 1 dated 1 August 1992
* Phosphate coat and oil to spec.
* Packed in packs of 250 to specification 307X

....

SIGNATURE BLOC

NOTES:

1. Please quote 'delivered our works'.
2. Tool costs are to be quoted separate from unit cost and if full cost or part cost.
3. Samples must be provided off production tools.
4. VAT to be shown separately.
5. Packaging costs to be included in unit cost.
6. Quotation should take note of terms and conditions shown overleaf.
7. Quote period of price stability.
8. Quotations to be considered must be received four working weeks from date of enquiry.

ORDER

TO: THE SUPPLIER   FROM: THE COMPANY

DATE: 1 September 1992   CONTACT: ____________

ORDER NO: 1500*   TEL NO: ____________

304–6150	Special Bolt	Level 1 (1 August 1992)	30p each
Part tool cost			£900.00

* Six samples off production tools to be delivered by 1 October 1992 (Subject to sample approval.)
* 1000 batch required 1 December 1992
* Packed in packs of 250 to specification 307X
* Price stable until 1 September 1994, as agreed by Mr J. Jones
* Phosphate coat and oil to specification
* Deliveries to schedule

....

SIGNATURE   COUNTER SIGNATURE

* ORDERS SHOULD BE NUMBERED CONSECUTIVELY BY THE PRINTER OF THE DOCUMENT.

PURCHASE ORDER AMENDMENT

TO: THE SUPPLIER

FROM: THE COMPANY

DATE: ____________________

CONTACT: ____________

NUMBER:557*

TEL NO: ____________

304–6150 Special Bolt

Please amend: Price of 30p each to 25p each with effect from all deliveries after 6 April 1993.

....
SIGNATURE BLOC

* PURCHASE ORDER AMENDMENTS SHOULD BE NUMBERED BY THE PRINTER TO A DIFFERENT SEQUENCE TO THE ORDERS.

4

FINANCIAL REPORTING, THE PURCHASING FORECAST AND THE CORPORATE PURCHASING PLAN

STANDARD COSTING

The majority of businesses need to establish a pricing structure which allows them to sell their products based on a sound and stable cost base. Very few companies can vary their price with every delivery, therefore the standard cost needs to be stabilized for as long as possible.

Typically, the company's standard costing system is made up of the following components:

1. material cost;
2. labour cost;
3. overhead cost.

The addition of these three components of cost add up to the:

4. works cost.

On to the works cost must be added:

5. sales costs, including advertising;
6. distribution costs;
7. profit margins.

The suppliers have the same cost components as the buyer's company has, thus the more you can learn about your own company's systems, the more easily you can understand your supplier's system.

Purchasing's greatest input is to the three components resulting in the works cost, and material cost is the highest percentage, typically material will contribute up to 70% of works cost.

In Chapter 3, a special bolt was ordered at 30p each and the buyer had negotiated two years' stability on price. So the price would not change in the new financial year.

HOW FINANCE/ACCOUNTS PREPARE STANDARDS

Let us assume that bolt 304–6150 is part of an assembly which comprises:

236-008	Pressing	£4.00	Last price agreed 1 January 1993
304-600	Spring	£3.00	Last price agreed 1 June 1993
304-200	Bearing	£1.00	Last price agreed 1 September 1992
304-6150	Special bolt	£0.30	Last price agreed 1 September 1992*

* Stable until 1 September 1994.

The company's financial year starts on 1 July each year and, at current prices, it will be seen that the material cost of the assembly is £8.30. (The new financial year runs from July 1993 to June 1994.)

The Finance department, who are responsible for producing the next financial year's standard cost, will ask the Purchasing Manager to tell them by how much all prices will change during the next financial year. With a 1 July start date, this process would start in the February/March period. This is to allow them to update the costs of all internal operations.

Clearly, the assessment of the next financial year's standard costs needs to be as accurate as possible because on the basis of the forecast standards depends the pricing structure and it may well be that marketing will say that a big increase cannot be reclaimed by increasing prices to the customer. In this case, it could be that redundancies have to be instigated to offset the increase, or the profit is reduced, or the product is phased out.

The need, then, is to be as precise as possible and standard setting time uncovers one of purchasing's biggest management burdens. The information you give here has got to be as true as you can make it.

PURCHASING'S FIRST CONSIDERATIONS (AN EXAMPLE)

If we consider the four suppliers who supply the components for the assembly, research tells us the following.

Supplier history

The pressing is supplied by the Able Company, a company with six divisions around the UK. Employees number 700, with a sales turnover of £80 000 000 per annum. The last price increase was an award of 5% in January 1993.

The spring is supplied by Bravo PLC, which has 80 employees and one factory based in Birmingham. Their sales turnover is £4 000 000. The last price increase awarded was 4% in June 1993.

The bearing is supplied by Sierra PLC, a Norwegian company with a factory in the north of England and factories all over Europe. The number of employees is 200 in the UK plant. Turnover is estimated at £6 000 000 for the UK plant and £700 000 000 world-wide. The last price increase was awarded in September 1992 for 6% (this could be driven by either political pricing or by economic effects).

Delta have 30 personnel and a turnover of £2.5 million. They are based in the Coventry area and have agreed to price stability for the coming financial year.

The purchasing history card (buying card) shows that the three suppliers, except Delta, ask for a price increase once a year and the last awards made were on the normal anniversary date.

Potential price increases

So, on the assumption that they will make their next request for an increase in the 1993 financial year, the percentage now needs to be established that each will be requesting.

Each of the three companies have a different commercial stance.

Able is a very advanced commercial organization and they are the owners of a reputation which is known throughout industry for going out of their way for big accounts – but they hammer the small turnovers; and our company's turnover with them is modest!

Bravo PLC have suffered in the recession and they are keen to keep their existing business. They nevertheless must try to stay viable and their dilemma will be simply how hard they dare press for a price increase.

Sierra PLC are a multinational who reward the national subsidiaries if they return a good profit by giving them capital allowances to improve their machine base and grow. Those that do not grow are allowed to wither on the vine. The management of the UK company are ambitious and wish to expand their customer base and for that they need to show they are successful profit-makers.

You have your lowest ultimate cost objective here in containing price increases – so you've got three interesting negotiations to come, two at least will be very firmly pressed.

Raw material movements

Interestingly, all four suppliers are big steel users, so if it were possible to know what content of their price to you is steel, then it would be possible to forecast what impact a steel price increase would put on their prices.

You spend £2 million per annum on steel yourself, thus you have (at least your steel buyer will have) probably as good a knowledge of steel prices for the next 12 months as your suppliers do.

You will know the steel industry's dilemmas and problems, their problems with the EC, import opportunities to bring in steel from outside the EC and so on, so a very realistic forecast for supplier steel price movement potential is easily obtainable. (Similar studies should be carried out on all other significant raw materials present in your 'buy'.)

It is highly worthwhile to know as precisely as you can what percentage of the supplier's price is made up of material cost. This could easily be between 60% and 70% of their selling price (depending on the product).

Labour movements

Labour costs vary through industry for a variety of reasons such as:

- actual labour rate;
- productivity;
- geographic area;

- male or female labour etc.

However, taking facts as they are, it is possible by some research to find out what the labour content is. In the industry we're discussing here, a good guess would be 15%, until you can obtain more precise information.

Overhead movements

This leaves the overhead, profit and packing element to deduce.

The following list includes the majority of elements:

rent;
rates;
lighting;
heating;
energy requirements;
canteen facilities;
NHI contributions;
pension fund;
transport;
telephones;
staff salaries etc.

In any given year, these costs move, most increase, some decrease, but of total selling price, overheads will constitute possibly no more than about 15%.

Material, labour and overhead

For the purpose of this exercise, it is not necessary to know what profit the suppliers are making; simply to assume that whatever percentage it is, will be taken into account by the material, labour and overhead split. For example, taking the pressing at £4.

The material would be	£2.80	(70%)
The labour would be	£0.60	(15%)
The overhead would be	£0.60	(15%)
	£4.00	

This is a broad-brush materials, labour and overheads (MLO) breakdown and can be assumed to represent the average of all Able's product, but ratios vary between suppliers and commodity groups and the more precise your information, the more accurate your forecasts become.

In later chapters, a more detailed description will be provided but, for standard setting, this is a safe routine to follow.

Commodity group forecasting of potential price increases

We also know from the study on supplier breakdown done in Chapter 1 that five pressing suppliers share £3 000 000 and that our spend with Able is £600 000 per annum.

Now that an MLO ratio has been established, it is possible to forecast the likely cost impacts that the supplier will suffer and assess from this the increase impact and timing they are likely to request in the form of a price increase.

Table Able as an example:

		MLO	1	2	3	4	5	6	7	8	9	10	11	12
Able Ltd	Ann T/O 600 000	70				3%								
		15												
		15												

Assuming that your steel buyer has told you that steel is expected to increase by 3% in Month 4 of your financial year, then 3% is noted above in Month 4.

Thus, 70% of Able's turnover will be uplifted by 3% if steel prices increase and all the components they supply will be similarly affected.

70% of £600 000 = £420 000 @ 3% = £12 600

This would be the 12 months effect; but since it occurs in the fourth month, there will only be an 8-month impact in the new financial year, e.g. £8400.

These two effects are referred to as fiscal year effect (£8400) and full year effect (£12 600).

The labour increase that the supplier will concede varies considerably from supplier to supplier – but if all else fails, it is always possible to establish what labour increase your company is likely to get – let's say 4%. So until you have better information, use your own company's forecast.

Now, labour awards are always an annual event in every company and always fixed with regard to date, so perhaps your supplier has an annual labour settlement in August which would be Month 2 in your financial year.

		MLO	1	2	3	4	5	6	7	8	9	10	11	12	F	F/Y
Able Ltd	Ann T/O 600 000	70				3%									£8.4	£12.6
		15		4%											£3.3	£ 3.6
		15														

Therefore, 15% of £600 000 = £90 000 × 4% – £3600 full year. Because the increase would occur in Month 2, 11/12 of the impact is in the fiscal year, therefore 3600/12 × 11 = £3300 – and this is the fiscal year effect.

Overhead

Many of the overhead factors are national and what affects The Company affects the suppliers too. Thus, if The Company is estimating 4% growth in overhead, then go with it for the suppliers until you can obtain specific information.

These increases go on throughout the year – but you could choose a mean month by which the majority will have happened – say Month 8.

Here the calculation is 4/12 of impact in fiscal.

Therefore, 4/12 × £3600 = £1200 (fiscal effect)
£3600 (full year effect)

Thus:

		MLO	1	2	3	4	5	6	7	8	9	10	11	12	F	F/Y
Able Ltd	Ann T/O 600 000	70				3%									£ 8.4	£12.6
		15		4%											£ 3.3	£ 3.6
		15								4%					£ 1.2	£ 3.6
															£12.9	£19.8

Thus, if this forecast is correct, Able Limited will face a fiscal effect in your financial year of £12 900. A full year effect (i.e. 12 months' impact) of £19 800 on their turnover with you.

$$= \frac{12\,900}{600\,000} \quad \text{fiscal} \quad = 2.15\%$$

and $\frac{19\ 800}{600\ 000}$ full year =3.3%

It is probable that Able, Bravo and Sierra would suffer similar uplifts in costs, apart from the offsets they can make by management intervention and action. You now have a very clear idea of what the most likely size of their annual price request will be in terms of percentage.

Communicating to finance – are you ready?

Finance are normally interested in the index change from Day 1 of Month 1, through to the last day of Month 12.

You could tell them that the most likely index change would be:

236-008	Pressing	£4.132	New standard (3.3%)
304-600	Spring	£3.099	New standard (3.3%)
304-200	Bearing	£1.033	New standard (3.3%)
304-6150	Special bolt	£0.30p	New standard (no increase)
Total cost of assembly		£8.564	New standard (material impact only)

Thus, the raw economic effect would move the current price from £8.30 to £8.564 – an index increase of 3.18%.

They would then uplift all the components supplied by this range of suppliers by the same percentages on all the assemblies in which these parts are used.

But, you also know the following.

1. That Able tend to hammer smaller accounts and yours is not one of their biggest. Can you contain/resist their price request?
2. That one of your profit improvement plans will be to reduce the five pressings suppliers down to, say, two. If you can achieve this, a condition of the movement would be a reduction in prices – not an increase!
3. You also know that you may be able to resist Bravo's request for an increase.
4. You know that Sierra may try to force you to pay a higher

increase than you can justify. (If you feel that you might be forced to concede – this should be entered in your losses forecast.)

5. You also know that the anniversary dates of the suppliers' price increases will contain the accumulation of those increases that have occurred since their last price discussion. (You do not pay for what has not yet happened!)

Assuming Able had not claimed last year's overhead and it was the same as this year's forecast, then if Able come in at their anniversary date of January, Month 7 of your financial year, they could claim 3.3% – but the fiscal effect would be low.

On the other hand, Bravo would be claiming an increase of 3.3% in Month 11 and you might be able to resist the increase.

Sierra will be the toughest and will be driving for their increase in September, your Month 3, which will give you a high fiscal! You can now forecast the date of these suppliers' price increases and the likely amount they will be claiming.

Preparation of the corporate purchasing plan

We are now approaching every purchasing manager's Waterloo – and what happens next depends on whether your name is the Duke of Wellington or Napoleon Bonaparte!

To tell Finance that all component costs would increase at index by 3.3% would be to lead them into a false position by over-calling the effect of economics and not giving any weight to the cost savings programmes you have already, or will have soon, in place and working.

It is quite probable that if your plans are successful, you could negotiate savings to offset the 3.3% increase making it zero growth or even reducing prices so that you achieve a (−2%), say, growth in prices.

Thus, you could be causing Finance to make a £1 250 000 over-estimate (e.g. 5% too high). So, you have yet another exercise to go through before you open your heart to Finance.

In Chapter 1, we established that 70 suppliers contribute 80% of your £25 000 000 spend. Although you've got 1200 suppliers, 1130 have only 20% of the spend between them and if the 80% can be controlled and forecast, the remainder can be assumed to be controllable in the same way.

So now a Purchasing Plan has to be prepared.

Taking the pressings suppliers of whom there are five, the situation at the beginning of the year is as follows.

Losses sheet*

Supplier	Ann T/O	MLO	1	2	3	4	5	6	7	8	9	10	11	12
Able	600 000								3.3%					
Baker	500 000	70									3.3%			
Jig	700 000	15										3.3%		
Sugar	300 000								3.3%					
Tare	900 000	15										3.3%		
Total Annual Turnover £3m	Fiscal								£12.0k		£ 4.1k	£ 8.8k		
	Full Year								£28.8k		£16.5k	£52.8k		

* With their anniversary dates plotted and Monthly Forecast Concessions also plotted.

Thus, Month 7 – the full year increase would be:

	Able	£19 800	(£8250 fiscal effect)
	Sugar	£ 9 000	(£3750 fiscal effect)
Month 9	Baker	£16 500	(£4125 fiscal effect)
Month 10	Jig	£23 100	(£3850 fiscal effect)
	Tare	£29 700	(£4950 fiscal effect)

You can now see that if you were to concede what economics could justify on a turnover of £3 million, you would concede £98 100 full year (index change) with a fiscal effect of £24 925 or 0.83% fiscal/ 3.3% full year.

By preparing this form for all your top 80% suppliers and the expected dates at which these claims would be conceded, you now have a theoretical losses sheet, with a bottom line.

Clearly, you will not concede a single penny without a struggle, but with the MLO work you have done which becomes more refined as experience grows, you know that any claim above 3.3% index is just not even worth considering and should be rejected out of hand.

Note, too, the profit contribution effect of just one month's delay in conceding an increase. The negotiation aspects are discussed later, but this exhibit will be referred to frequently. Clearly, the later the fiscal effect, the better the company profit situation.

Each chief buyer and his or her buyers should prepare a similar sheet based on the economic considerations, i.e. materials, labour, overhead in each group and which you must involve yourself with them on each commodity range. (Each range may show different rates and times of increase.)

The savings plan

Next comes the savings plan. Here we are seeking to produce a plan to offset (at least) the increases which will occur if we do nothing, also on each commodity group.

It is almost 100% certain that the suppliers in the pressings group would each like to increase their turnover, not only does it allow them to get the benefits of greater production, but it provides growth potential, their shareholders like it and the labour like it. This will be true in most other commodity groups.

Therefore, you should be able to redistribute the work among a smaller number of suppliers. This increases their turnover with the company and it increases your 'clout' with them. Because you become a more important customer the benefits you need to satisfy the MD's requirements become a condition of your giving some of these suppliers more business at the expense of the others.

Timing within the purchasing plan

As an example, your chief buyer and buyers on the pressing section will have to prepare an enquiry which lists all the pressings that are supplied with drawings and specifications etc., and then launched to all five companies. (The timing of this massive exercise has to be fitted in with all their other tasks.) Simultaneously, the other sections will be carrying out parallel exercises on their commodity groups.

The suppliers quote, the buying staff prepare quotation analyses. Recommendations are made and a sourcing decision is made.

To move the items to the new suppliers, obtain sample approval etc., will take from beginning to end some four to five months to do – add on some time for 'funk factor' delays – usually elevated to 'management judgement' and you could assume completion of the operation by, say, Month 10.

Conservatively, you should obtain something in the order of a 4% reduction on current turnovers, thus a savings sheet is prepared as below.

Savings forecast

Supplier	Ann T/O	1	2	3	4	5	6	7	8	9	10	11	12	F	F/Y
Able	600 000														
Baker	500 000														
Jig	700 000	Resource to two suppliers only									4%			£30k	£120k
Sugar	300 000														
Tare	900 000														
	£3m													1%	4%

Thus, your net plan for the new financial year on pressings is:

Percentage terms

Losses	(0.83%)	fiscal	(3.27%)	full year
Savings	1.00%	fiscal	4.00%	full year
Net saving	0.17%	fiscal	0.73%	full year

Communication of corporate purchasing plan to finance/accounting

On the assumption that your other sections report the same percentages of potential losses and savings as the pressing section have done, their reports would show that the bottom line total would be:

£24 000 000 turnover (less capital)

Losses	(0.83%)	fiscal	(3.27%)	full year
Savings	1.00%	fiscal	4.00%	full year
Net saving	0.17%	fiscal	0.73%	full year

Or, in cash terms:

Losses	(£199 200)	fiscal	(£784 800)	full year
Savings	£240 000	fiscal	£960 000	full year
Net saving	£ 40 800	fiscal	£175 200	full year

So that, at minimum, you would be planning to offset all inflation and provide a 0.73% index saving.

Prudence might dictate that you state 'no change to standards' for the new financial year.

In fact, the savings would be much greater than those shown above because the 'Losses' assume that you would concede the forecast increases in Months 7, 9 and 10, almost certainly the increases would not arise at all, as you would be transferring the work. Also, in many other cases, you will be able to resist increases which are claimed; or reduce or delay them, while still making the planned savings.

THE PURCHASING STRATEGY

As manager of the department, you will be keeping a very close eye on the losses forecast to minimize the losses and to pump up the savings. If you use this approach you can have confidence that Finance are getting the most realistic forecast you can give them, and your Corporate Plan is your way of ensuring that you maintain or improve the forecast and achieve your strategic goals.

There is an interesting aspect to this because the whole department is now committed to achieving or bettering the plan. A common objective exists in which the buyers, the chief buyers and you are all committed. Targeting of achievement is easily measurable and because everyone has had an input, there is a real sense of 'go get it Tiger' which is very gratifying and productive.

The PPV (purchase price variance) report

You have told Finance that there will be no change to standards during the new financial year.

How it works

Accounting produce a purchase price variance report monthly which compares actual price versus standard of all receipts during the month. Taking the example of the pressings, in Month 7, you might have had to concede £28 800 (i.e. £2400 per month to Able and Sugar). In Month 9, £16 500 (i.e. £1375 per month to Baker) and in Month 10, £52 800 (i.e. £4400 per month to Jig and Tare).

(Hopefully your plans to reduce cost on this commodity are so advanced that you can have resourced these materials before the anniversary dates or you have told the suppliers you are resourcing and the increases will not be paid.)

But, assuming you were running late, then in the case of Able and Sugar, you had conceded the 3.3% increase then each item they supply would have been uplifted by this percentage and a PPV report would be issued.

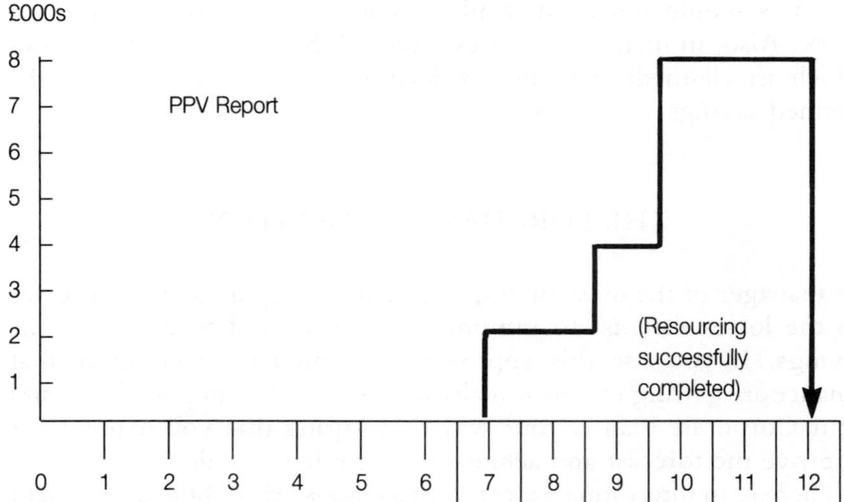

Increases to price (£000s)

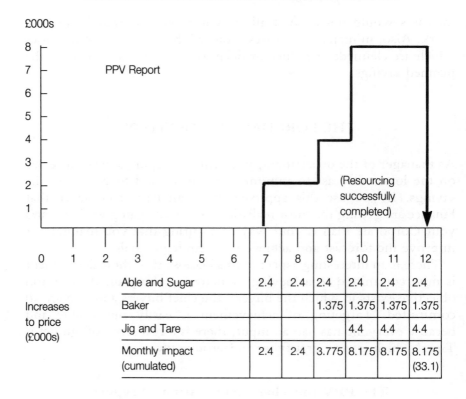

	7	8	9	10	11	12
Able and Sugar	2.4	2.4	2.4	2.4	2.4	2.4
Baker			1.375	1.375	1.375	1.375
Jig and Tare				4.4	4.4	4.4
Monthly impact (cumulated)	2.4	2.4	3.775	8.175	8.175	8.175 (33.1)

The report cumulates each increase monthly so that your PPV graph could look like the example above. This report should be itemized by accounting showing all items where actual price is above standard and/or last price paid.

The example shows that delay in carrying out the resourcing exercise until, say, the 12th month has cost £33 100 and although you will end up comfortably below standard, there has been a significant loss of profit.

This document is an excellent cross-check to your plan performance and it forms part of your own plan management. It is also one of the bases for your monthly meetings with the boss!

While on the subject of the PPV, the itemized excesses against standard (or current order) will also include other less immediately recognizable items.

Some of these include:

1. transport costs added to supplier invoice when order states delivery paid;
2. packaging costs added to supplier invoice when order states packaging paid;

3. genuine mistakes on suppliers' invoices – such as wrong extensions, wrong unit prices etc;
4. price not as order etc.

All these costs are also shown in the cumulated over standard payments column, and each has to be resolved and corrected.

This part of the PPV report is a pain – because if you don't act, the company is losing money – but, in most cases, the individual costs are small and seem hardly worth your buyer's time to resolve.

Nevertheless, the discipline has to be firmly in place to know what has caused the purchase price variance and to correct the error.

Reporting savings and losses against the purchasing plan

Savings and losses are both measured against last price paid within purchasing. This is (to purchasing) the *real* world.

Thus, the forecast savings and losses forecasts can be updated monthly, and a net performance calculated, since these are based on actual prices. This report should form part of the Monthly Management Report (Chapter 13) and be circulated to Marketing.

The company (Finance, Accounting and Sales) are more interested in savings against standard, because this is where they see the effect of Purchasing's work in works costs to sales.

The discomfort in purchasing derives from the fact that because Purchasing have tremendous plans to reduce prices on supplier orders, they have said that there will be no change to standards. Thus, if Purchasing achieve all their plans and the index change is '0', they have made no savings against standard!

Of course they have, because they've offset all inflation effect, but it is not immediately visible.

Nevertheless, it is highly worthwhile that each time a price movement (either up or down) is being worked on, the buyer checks the standard. Often, due to the detail within negotiations, prices change against standard and these changes should be reported.

Thus, the wise purchasing manager reports two separate events:

1. savings and losses against actual prices paid;
2. savings and losses against standard.

In this chapter, it has been demonstrated that before an accurate standard can be set, Purchasing must have their economic forecast in place, plans prepared and timings established. If, for any reason, individual standards have to be changed, these can be done by exception.

It has also demonstrated that different suppliers will behave differently under the same economic stimuli.

This entire process takes very careful managing both in the forecasting and planning stage, and in the monitoring and motivational stages which are continuous throughout the year.

Some purchasing managers try to treat standard setting as a five-minute dash through a computer tab, showing current prices and push it back to Accounting with quick amendments made alongside some items.

Don't be one of them, because as the financial year goes on, they get buried by PPVs and are constantly trying to explain the differences. This doesn't do their reputations any good at all!

And as far as The Company is concerned, everybody is consumed with doubt and management confidence is dented.

In the worst cases, MDs have been heard to say 'we want to know whether we've made a profit or a loss, but we won't know for sure, until the year end figures are produced'.

Their purchasing managers have short – but interesting careers!

5

THE RECRUITMENT PROCESS

There are considerable differences in the way various companies select their new staff.

Probably you and the personnel manager have sifted through a great number of CVs and graded the majority as not suitable, another group as possibles, and a third group as the most likely candidates.

Personnel will have sent the majority a nice letter thanking them for their interest, the most likely candidates have been given appointments to attend for interview and the middle group are 'on hold' depending on the results of the first set of interviewees.

THE FIRST INTERVIEW

In order to save time, often the personnel manager goes through the facts of the candidate's CV. This includes date of birth, current address, married or single, educational qualifications and a quick run through the candidate's employment history.

From this the personnel manager will attempt to glean four or five facts, as follows.

1. Is the candidate 'flannelling'?
2. What sort of personality does the candidate have?
3. Is the candidate the sort of person Personnel think should be in Purchasing?
4. Current, or last, salary and expectations.

Before wheeling the candidate in to see you, the personnel manager will give you a quick summary of his or her findings/opinions.

FORMING AN ASSESSMENT

You have, no doubt, read and absorbed the appropriate job application and you will have a sense of the personal qualities of the folk you are hoping to recruit and the way they are progressing through their chosen profession.

First impressions count for a lot and the candidates' dress, haircut, shirt, tie and shoes all start to form an impression. Whether we like it or not, there is a uniform which people choose to wear to signify themselves and if that uniform doesn't fit the bill, the candidate is already in difficulties.

Clearly, many people are nervous in interview and many buyers of all ranks confess always to feeling nervous when they are starting a negotiation, for example, or when making a presentation.

1. Probably, if your candidates don't look nervous, they feel it, so your first question should be designed to put them at ease, something like, 'Did you have a good journey here today?'

   Asking about the candidate's current job will put the candidate further at ease and it is here, by asking leading questions, you start to learn what real authority he or she has.

   The candidate may say, 'On our section we have made a considerable impact on reducing the number of suppliers we used to use'. (Listen for that 'we' – it could be modesty – many buyers are very coy about blowing their own trumpets – or the candidate really may mean 'we'.)
2. In the above case, the right question is, 'OK, a good section effort, but what was your role in this operation?' The candidate may then describe clearly and succinctly his/her role in the reduction of suppliers and you can judge several things from the response.
   (a) Does the candidate use his or her own initiative?
   (b) Does the candidate just carry out orders?
   (c) What criteria did they use to get rid of the suppliers and who was the initiator of the criteria?

   You should look for the 'mover' if the applicant is aiming for a chief buyership with you, look for one who initiated sub-exercises within the whole operation without having to be told.
3. Another question which is very useful in revealing the character of the candidate is, 'Would you please tell me what negotiation, or other operation, have you carried out – that you are most proud of?'

   Many candidates have something they are proud of; some will

be turning round a desperate supply situation, others breaking a monopoly, others still, a very tricky negotiation which came right only because of some action they took themselves.

In the reply to this question, test the candidate's method of thinking through the approach to the problem; the action itself and what was the candidate's fall-back situation.

The candidate's action could have been a knee-jerk reaction in line with previous training, but much more to his/her credit is the reasoning process used to formulate the plan.

The reason for checking what fall-back situation the candidate had is that there are old buyers and there are bold buyers – but you never meet an old, bold buyer. You'll meet old buyers who are very willing to take risks – but with carefully thought out fall-back positions.

Even in a negotiation where there is a failure to agree, the good negotiator always leaves a chink of light either to use him or herself or for the opponent to use, so that the failure to agree is not permanent and the opportunity exists to reopen the matter.

There are few candidates who can't think of anything they are proud of. (After a few moments of silence, and nothing of interest from the candidate, move on to the next question – but this is a serious black mark.)

4. A useful question to follow with is designed to find out what the buyer knows about the items he or she buys now. 'The materials that you buy now are used in what type of end product?'
5. From this answer, you move on to ask, 'How do you establish the lowest ultimate cost in your buying activities?' This should lead you into finding out how well the candidate knows the items he/she buys.

   The buyer (of whatever grade) cannot know too much about their items and should know what the raw materials are, how the raw material is converted into the product he/she buys, how it is packed and delivered, and what inventory is held and so on.
6. From this question, you can lead the candidate to give you some opinions on production control, manufacturing, design engineering etc.

   The candidate may be very scathing about some or all of these areas – what you are looking for is a constructive analysis of what these departments should do.

   If, after the candidate has stopped getting red in the face, you get a clear idea of what the candidate feels they should do – you may find you have a very useful ally to have on your side.

A test of your own management style

7. Your next question should be along the lines of the candidate's belief of the type of relationship a buying department should have with its suppliers.

   There are a range of responses here and you should take careful note of the candidate's answer, which could be as follows.

   (a) 'So far as I'm concerned, suppliers are just in it for the money – so I pick 'em up and drop 'em as I please.'

   (b) 'I believe we should form a partnership and work together to achieve the best price, delivery and so on.'

   (c) 'They should be treated entirely at arm's length and we should never show any friendliness and select only those suppliers who supply right time, right material, right price, right quality etc.'

   Surprisingly, all three of these responses are exact reflections of the way various companies do business, and the replies are typical for the buyers who come out of these companies and are demonstrating the way they have been trained.

   (The writer has a high preference for a position between (b) and (c), but you will have to consider what your management style will be and which type of department you wish to run.)

8. A question which is a little difficult to pose is to try to assess the allegiance of the candidates to their employer and their willingness to work until they drop if it is in the company's interest to do so.

   You don't want 'nine to five' people.

9. Following this question, it is necessary to know if the candidate is willing to travel any time, anywhere and this is best led into by asking if they have any experience in buying overseas. Some buyers may give the impression that they like to have all their suppliers within 40 miles of the factory.

   The good buyer will buy from the best source almost without exception, wherever in the world that supplier can be found.

   You don't want parochial buyers!

10. If the candidates are applying for a chief buyer post, then you should turn your attention to their abilities in staff-management and training.

    Again, you may have your own ideas on this, but if the candidate's ideas are positive and constructive (even if they differ from yours), there is an opportunity for you to debate this difference with them to test their mettle.

At some stage in the interview, you should take an opposite view from the one the candidate clearly holds. By doing this and noting how the reply is presented; and if you've got the candidate slightly annoyed, so much the better, since this is a good test of the candidate as an independent thinker who is willing to support their views. The introduction of controlled friction into any interview is vital because you don't want sycophants – but when the discussion is completed, the candidate should be capable of carrying out your final decision with a good heart – after all, you'd be the boss!

Up to now, apart from providing questions and observing the replies, the candidate has done most of the talking, which is as it should be. Ideally, now you should talk about the company and explain the role that is being competed for.

11. Then allow the candidate time to ask you some questions, these questions often also giving you a guide to their mind and personality.
12. Finally, you should ask the candidate why they want to join the company. When this is explained you then have the opportunity to say that you will be in contact again and show the candidate out.

There are 12 questions that have been asked by you with some sub-clauses and will probably have taken about 45 minutes to complete.

A good tip is to list the questions and mark each reply out of 10, not forgetting to write the candidate's name on the sheet. This gives you a basis for judging the candidates on even ground.

When the next candidate comes in you should ask the same questions, and also note the chemistry which exists between you and each candidate.

A PROVISIONAL ASSESSMENT

If you and the candidate have had a good rapport and the personnel manager is not too anti, then you've got a good possibility there. You should beware the personnel manager saying that candidate A is 'too aggressive' and candidate B is 'too tough' – you need people like this. Personnel's fear is that they will cause friction. Your hope is that they will! Beneficial friction is a very powerful motivating tool for buyers.

Using the processes described so far, you may end up with, say, six short-list candidates for the four chief buyer roles.

By the specialities that they have already had experience of, it will almost certainly be possible to allocate each one to one of your areas of responsibility, perhaps with a few adjustments here and there.

THE SHORT-LIST INTERVIEWS

Since these chief buyer candidates will be your first line, it may be that your MD may wish to interview them with you and the personnel manager together as a panel.

If the panel process is to be used, your role should be not exactly the 'prisoner's friend', but the other two panellists may be hostile and since, if the candidate is successful, he or she will be working for you, a little kindness is not forbidden.

In order that you can test the candidates' capability, it is very helpful if you give them a case study to discuss.

It doesn't have to be too complicated. You could start by saying, 'I would like you to imagine that you have to source an engine block casting. Could you explain how you would go about finding a suitable source?' When the sourcing procedure has been described, you may then ask why the candidate didn't use a foreign source and, if they did, why didn't the candidate use a UK source? The explanation should demonstrate a firmness of decision.

Possibly, if it hasn't been covered already – ask how the supplier will ensure quality? The explanation should show a good appreciation of the necessities for quality procedures.

Then, since the casting has to be machined, how would the candidate decide whether it should be machined in-house or at an external supplier? This leads to a discussion of make versus buy processes.

The candidate should be getting mentally active by now and your colleagues can either interrupt with technical questions of the type you have been asking – or, indeed, their own favourite questions.

If the candidate is handling all of you well and pleasantly, and demonstrating good professional skills, give another push by saying, 'The patterns have been made and the supplier rings you one morning to say they've declared themselves bankrupt and the receiver is in. Your deadline for samples and production are next month. What are you going to do?'.

Chief buyers work under pressure and, if in an interview situation, your candidate demonstrates coolness under fire and uses good knowledge of a range of skills, you've found one of your new employees.

A DECISION ONLY YOU CAN MAKE

Assuming the selected candidates have to give a month's notice before they can join you, you now have another decision to take.

Do you personally want to recruit the buyers and the purchasing assistants with the aid of the personnel department or do you want to wait until the chief buyers are aboard and let them make the selection? There are arguments of equal weight for both choices.

You know more about the company than your newly recruited chief buyers will know for several months – on the other hand, the teams will report to their chief buyers and chemistry is important in having cohesive teams in place quickly.

In a perfect world, you could do the preliminary interviews with personnel and let the newly joined chief buyers make a final choice. Yet you are driven to get 'bums on seats' as quickly as possible.

Under the circumstances, the writer would recruit the buyers and purchase assistants with the aid of personnel, and have them joining the company if possible at the same time as the chief buyers.

Now this is a tremendous load for a newly positioned purchasing manager to undertake.

USE OF CONSULTANTS

There are some very good purchasing consultancy and recruitment firms with first-rate track records who could undertake the advertising (if they didn't have suitable people on their books already) and do all the preliminary interviews, and produce a short list of suitable candidates for you to make a final selection. (They can also help in providing training, sourcing advice, management selection, cost investigation etc.)

Here we are then, several weeks later, and the new people are joining the department next week.

FINAL PREPARATIONS FOR THE NEW RECRUITS

What should you have prepared so that your new recruits can become functional as quickly as possible?

- office accommodation
- furniture
- telephones/VDUs/fax/telex
- forms and stationery

(See Chapter 3)

- basic procedures and policies (See Chapter 6)
- coffee and tea facilities
- canteen facilities
- conference room
- car parking
- salary payment etc.
- internal telephone directory
- accounting codes for expense budgets/purchasing codes etc.

You should also be making a presentation to the heads of all other departments, and perhaps their departmental members too, in which you describe what you are doing and what you are hoping to achieve.

If you have established a personal knowledge base which covers the points raised in Chapters 1 to 4, you will be able to quantify your major tasks for the first 12 months. You will have to have their co-operation in order to succeed, so you should also demonstrate how you, in return, will be setting out to serve your 'customers' and to improve their performance.

It is very difficult not to be 'up tight' and defensive in these presentations because the world is full of cynics and NIMBYs ('Not in my back yard') and they always seem to pack presentations like this.

To keep control, it is a good tip to use overhead projectors which show how much the company needs Purchasing and, if the slides embarrass the viewers a little, it takes the edge off their cynicism.

Another aspect that you should prepare for is what you will say to the new personnel as they arrive.

It is likely that none of your staff will know each other so you'll have to carry out introductions, so each chief buyer can get to know his or her own team, and the department all get to know each other well in order to work closely together.

One useful tip here is to assemble the chief buyers in the conference room and show them the presentation you made to the heads of the other departments.

Before doing this, provide them with a piece of card on which they write their names so that the others can see it and let each tell the others something about their background history with other companies, and so on.

When the department is all together, make the same presentation (simplified perhaps) to the whole group.

THE INTERNAL MANAGEMENT MEETING

You should also set aside a morning (preferably the same one each week) for an internal management meeting.

The agenda should be broad enough to allow the chief buyers a considerable input and to discuss in open forum what they are currently dealing with, what difficulties they are encountering and how *you* can help them.

If you set, say, Friday at 9.00 a.m. as the time for the purchasing meeting, your staff can plan to ensure that they will be 'on the ground' and it helps the whole department if you also are always present for these meetings.

So, finally, each individual should receive a pack which contains a potted company history, the names of the members of the department by section, how to obtain stationery, car parking, method of paying salary, terms of employment, accounting codes etc., on arrival.

UNION MEMBERSHIP

Purchasing is the supply arm of the company and is also the biggest influence on cost in the organization. If Purchasing fails in its objectives, the damage done can be very long term in its effects.

Union strategy can be aimed at forcing a company to negotiate by preventing a small vital part of the company performing its function, thus preventing the whole company from functioning. Purchasing can be a prime target.

During the 1970s and the early 1980s, there was closed-shop operating in many plants and the purchasing staff *had* to join a union before they could be employed.

Many buyers were called out because of a strike in the clerical unions and great damage was done because they were out.

THE PROFESSIONAL GRADES

The way that eligibility for union membership was defined to avoid this was by the introduction of the 'professional grades'. Thus, accountants, designers, purchasing people etc. could be termed 'professional' and were not – as part of their terms and conditions of employment – allowed to act as union members, although if they wished, they could still be members.

The criteria was broadly accepted by defining the move to professional at the point at which the buyer was a qualified member of the Institute of Purchasing and Supply. In other companies, it was defined by professional grades which were agreed between management and unions.

While the whole union/management scene changed as the 1980s wore on, a wise purchasing manager should still determine with Personnel how a division can be made and at what level in your department that division should be made so that all essential services can be maintained in the event of a return to the management/union friction of the 1970s and early 1980s.

Those two decades may have been an aberration, but who knows?

6

POLICIES, PROCEDURES, DEPARTMENTAL BUDGETS AND TIMING CONTROL

The *Collins Dictionary* gives two relevant descriptions of 'policy'.

1. A plan of action adopted or pursued by an individual, government, party or business etc.
2. Wisdom, prudence, shrewdness or sagacity.

Clearly, as head of a department, required to take on the role of supply at the lowest ultimate cost, you need to define the policy or policies under which your department will function.

Also, in order that these policies are adhered to, you need a set of procedures which the department use to implement the policies.

One of the prime requirements is that you and your staff are performing to a strict code of ethics. Because you are a fiscal department, potential suppliers may attempt to persuade you to do business with them by offering inducements.

In 1976, the Institute of Purchasing and Supply issued a Code of Ethics (slightly abridged here), which you may wish to employ as your first policy statement, and which has stood the test of time.

CODE OF ETHICS

1. Purchasing personnel shall never use their authority or office for personal gain, and shall seek to uphold the standing of the profession by:

(a) maintaining an unimpeachable standard of integrity in all their business relationships both inside and outside the organization in which they are employed;
(b) fostering the highest possible standards of professional competence among those for whom they are responsible;
(c) optimizing the use of resources for which they are responsible to provide the maximum benefit to their employing organization;
(d) Complying with both the letter and the spirit of
    (i) the law of the country in which they practise,
    (ii) such guidance on professional practice as may be issued by properly constituted bodies including the Institute of Purchasing and Supply,
    (iii) contract obligations;
(e) rejecting any business practice which might reasonably be deemed improper.

In applying these precepts, purchasing personnel should follow the guidance set out below.

(a) Declaration of interest
Any personal interest which may impinge or might reasonably be deemed by others to impinge on any purchasing personnel's impartiality in any matter relevant to his or her duties should be declared.

(b) Confidentiality and accuracy of information
The confidentiality of information received in the course of duty should be respected and should never be used for personal gain; information given in the course of duty should be fair and true, and never designed to mislead.

(c) Competition
While bearing in mind the advantages to the purchasing personnel's employing organization of maintaining a continuing relationship with a supplier, any arrangement which might, in the long term, prevent the effective operation of fair competition should be avoided.

(d) Business gifts
Business gifts other than items of very small intrinsic value, such as business diaries or calendars, should not be accepted.

(e) Hospitality
Modest hospitality is an accepted courtesy of a business relationship. However, the recipient should not allow him or herself to reach a position whereby he or she might be or might by others be deemed to have been influenced in making a business decision as a consequence of accepting

such hospitality; the frequency and scale of hospitality accepted should not be significantly greater than the recipient's employer would be likely to provide in return.
(f) When it is not easy to decide what is, and what is not acceptable in terms of gifts and hospitality, the offer should be declined or advice sought from the employee's superior.

The second policy that needs to be put in place is:

2. Responsibility of Purchasing
   (a) Purchasing has the ultimate responsibility for all purchase and supply commitments. Any delegation of purchasing authority to other departments should be covered by specific written instructions to all involved personnel from the head of Purchasing and his or her chief.
   (b) The head of Purchasing has the responsibility for establishment and maintenance of purchasing policies and procedures, records and forms which should be made available to all interested personnel.
   (c) The head of Purchasing or his or her delegate should review and approve prior to the award of business the buyer's quotation analysis when an award cannot be made on a competitive basis, in conformance with established procedures.
   (d) The head of the department or his or her delegate should audit from time to time all buying operations under his or her control to ensure compliance with policies and procedures.
3. The Purchasing function
   (a) Maintain records of price histories by part number and supplier, records of negotiation dates etc. In the event of supply difficulties to take necessary action together with production control/industrial relations/engineering etc. to ensure uninterrupted supply for production.
   (b) Be familiar with all Government Acts and laws national and international which affect purchasing.
   (c) Attempt to promote good community and supplier relations at all times.
   (d) Work in close co-operation with Finance/Accounts. No one individual should have sole jurisdiction for a given transaction from inception through to authorization for payment. Purchasing commitments should conform to the provisions of the established inventory and commitment control practices.
   (e) Keep informed of future requirements for new parts, materials

and tooling. This advance information should be used to develop potential suppliers and to survey possible new materials, methods and processes which may reduce costs and/or improve quality of performance.

(f) Confer with associates and other departments in critical evaluation of new ideas, products, methods, processes and expenditures. Continuous effort should be made to reduce costs without sacrifice of quality through such activities as competitive enquiry, value analysis and price analysis.

(g) Explore all markets domestic and world for new sources, products and processes, and be alert to new ideas and suggestions.

(h) To ensure that all deliveries are made to meet scheduled and other requirement dates. If suppliers fail to meet delivery dates where 'time is of the essence' (as in most orders), they should be replaced with more efficient sources.

Further policies should be issued covering:

4. Relationships with suppliers

The main points are:

The relationship must be scrupulously balanced in that:

(a) for Purchasing, this means buying at the lowest ultimate cost;

(b) for the supplier, this means the assurance of fair and courteous treatment, and a high standard of ethics in all transactions. Loyalty and impartiality must be combined but the best assurance of continued loyalty is continued competitiveness;

(c) the supplier must receive a fair price for his or her product.

5. Purchasing approvals

Purchasing can only accept purchasing requisitions or other instructions to buy from properly authorized personnel. An approval system for signature levels in the department must be created and maintained.

Purchasing should maintain a current signature file which covers both aspects.

6.–9. Quotations

The following steps should be applied to all transactions including regular, or annual renewal of blanket orders etc., for production, service, capital and consumable items.

In instances where these steps are not followed, records must be noted accordingly and the action should be approved by the head of Purchasing.

7. Selection of sources
   (a) Purchasing should develop and maintain a list of approved suppliers broad enough to ensure that a competitive cross section of the market will receive enquiries. Competitiveness is designated as supplying at the lowest ultimate cost (which includes timely deliveries).
   (b) Competitive written quotations should normally be received against each enquiry. If in cases of urgency, telephoned quotations are solicited, they should be supported as soon as possible with written quotations.
   (c) Potential suppliers should be formally surveyed by Purchasing and Quality Control prior to their being accepted for inclusion in the list of approved suppliers.
   (d) Due to the technical or specialized nature of certain requirements, the co-operation of other departments is required in producing specifications and the use of specialized suppliers.

       These specifications should not be written so that only one supplier can quote and purchasing should ensure that it is possible to obtain quotations from more than one source.

       No contact with such suppliers should be made by the assisting departments, except with the approval of Purchasing.
8. Raising enquiries

   The enquiry should contain:
   - complete specifications
   - all drawings
   - forecast quantities
   - delivery requirements
   - tool ownership

   Terms and conditions should appear with the enquiry.

   Except in low value purchases, a quotation analysis should always be prepared.
   (a) Normally, the lowest quote should receive the business – but if the quote is patently too low, it should be checked out and discarded, if in error.
   (b) Dual or single sourcing. Normally, single sourcing provides the best unit price result (highest volume) and, where tooling is involved, it is an expensive business to lay down two sets of tooling.

       Supply protection is most often achieved by inventory protection precautions.

In the event that second sourcing is recommended, it should not be implemented unless the decision has the concurrence of the departmental head.

9. Purchase orders

(a) The purchasing order is the medium for conveying all information relative to each transaction and it must be prepared in such a way that the supplier has no doubt as to its requirements. It should contain:

- part number, description and latest specification;
- if necessary, the service to be performed and all the information necessary for punctual delivery to the desired location;
- the supplier's correct name and address, price, payment terms, quantities, account distribution and any other relevant information;
- not forgetting the terms and conditions!

Orders and purchase order amendments should be numbered by the printers (this is to ensure full traceability and to permit audit).

(b) Types of purchase order:

(i) Firm order

This is complete within itself and requires no further releases or instructions. If the quantity is to be dispatched in part lots, the shipping schedule should form part of the order.

(ii) Blanket order

These are issued to define the price at which the supplier will sell and the buyer buy for an agreed period of time.

The instrument of a blanket order is a schedule issued for a period of firm requirement and a period of tentative requirement, say two months firm and three tentative.

The tentative section can be for information only or for the acquisition of raw material. It does not give the supplier the authority to manufacture beyond the amount in the firm commitment.

The schedule should be reissued monthly.

(iii) Time and materials orders

These should include a definition of labour hours and material cost. The buyer should establish that the rates quoted are competitive and that records should show evidence to this effect. Any expense items which are to be included as overhead should be specified. Any retention sum pending audit of completion should be specified on the order.

(iv) In some cases it may be necessary to execute a formal contract in addition to the appropriate purchasing order. The terms and conditions of the company order are meant to embrace all aspects of the transaction, but in many cases cannot.

In which case, a draft contract is to be raised by purchasing and confirmed by the company's legal authority.

10. Right to audit supplier's records

Where purchase orders are placed on such terms as:

(a) time and material;
(b) cost plus fixed fee;
(c) cost plus incentive fee;
(d) price to be determined.

The supplier must ensure that his or her records will stand a proper audit and a front of order clause such as:

> 'By acceptance of this order (or contract), the supplier grants to the company access to all pertinent ledgers, payroll data, books, records and any other documents for the purpose of auditing the charges relating to this contract, and retaining all documentation for 12 months after completion of the transaction.'

Finance/Accounts will, together with Purchasing, decide how this audit is to be carried out.

11. Transport terms

Normally, for domestic transport to the company, the most usual clause is 'delivered our works, carriage paid, packing included'.

For international transport, INCOTERMS are employed.

These terms are available from the Board of Trade and define a series of terms varying from:

- *Ex-works* (EXW) where the buyer pays all charges including packing, transport to the docks or airport, shipping, insurance and dock charges, Customs duties and transport to their works.
- *FOB* which is 'free on board ship' and all subsequent costs are the buyers.
- *CIF* which is 'cost, insurance and freight' where the seller covers all costs to named port of destination.

Selection of the right INCOTERM saves cost. (There are more than a dozen different INCOTERMS.)

12. Administrative responsibilities of purchasing

    Purchasing should hold themselves responsible for:

    (a) bringing to the attention of the appropriate personnel instances where the price of a new part exceeds the price of the part it replaces. Changes may be suggested by purchasing which will either prevent or minimize the anticipated cost impact;
    (b) work with quality and reliability functions and communicate. Quality = reliability standards to suppliers;
    (c) take an active part in recommending make versus buy actions;
    (d) to co-operate with other departments on value analysis exercises and to offer for test and possible use new products, materials etc.;
    (e) initiate standardization exercises;
    (f) work closely with material handling to ensure that most economical packaging specifications and methods are being authorized;
    (g) advise authorizers of requisitions of any cost savings that could be made by different timing and quantity scheduling of orders or by material substitution or by source change;
    (h) be alert to pass upwards information which senior personnel in the organization should be made aware of;
    (i) search out methods to reduce inventory without prejudicing supply or increasing cost.

The preceding 12 policies will give you a good start in formulating the procedures by which the policies will be implemented and your department will start to take a cohesive form.

Previous chapters have outlined the form of the enquiry, the quotation analysis, the order, terms and conditions, and by attaching as Appendices these documents to the foregoing policies, your people will have a very good idea of where you want them to go.

DEPARTMENTAL BUDGETS

This is another part of the administration aspect of Purchasing management which allows the manager to keep a tight control on expenditure. During the run-up to the new financial year, you will be required to submit a budget for the new year.

Depending on the depth to which finance/accounting exert control, you will be given a set of cost categories to forecast.

The areas most likely are:

1. salaries by grade;
2. merits forecast and timing;
3. travel costs;
4. stationery requirements;
5. overtime;
6. training;
7. publications;
8. extra requirements such as typewriters, VDUs, telephones etc.;
9. increased headcount, i.e. one new typist.

You will then make a forecast over 12 months of the expenditure on all of these aspects at least.

One thing to beware of. Let us say that you had planned to send three buyers off on a course during the first quarter at a cost of £2000 and, due to any number of reasons, couldn't send them. Accounting (always anxious to reduce departmental budgets) will assume that you no longer want this sum and will take it out of your budget. Will they put it back when you protest? Not likely!

So, as soon as you find yourself in a situation like the one described, bang out a fast budget revision putting that £2000 further down the year, when you will be able to send the buyers on their course.

Accounting should, at the end of each month, report to you your actual spend month by month.

If you had forecast total overtime at £5000 per month, this appears a large sum but with a salary bill approaching £300 000 per annum, £60 000 per annum of overtime (and considering it is paid at premium rates) is not a great deal of hours and the accountants say you have spent only £4000 – what do you do?

The writer would bang out a budget revision assuming an extra £1000 at the last month of the financial year – otherwise you might lose it.

If those in accounting in your organization are like some of those in the writer's experience, it forces you to play 'silly beggers' too. If they are more reasonable, then of course don't bother because they should also show you cumulatively each month how much you've got left and how many months to run.

But what if you're exceeding your £5000 per month forecast? Your questions must be as follows.

1. Did you forecast too low?
2. Is someone, or a group, caning the overtime?
3. Have events changed since you did your budget?

Clearly, you've got to take action.

Curiously, if experience shows that £60 000 in overtime is about right, at time and a half that means that if you deployed £40 000 on salaries and extra heads, you could do without the overtime *and* get more work done and save £20 000.

The good manager should always be thinking along these lines and looking for ways to make the department more cost-effective – but without turning into a 'nit-picker'!

TIMING CONTROL

In and amongst all the processes going on in Purchasing there is the backbone process of order and requisition placing.

It's probable that there will be several different ways by which requisitions, releases, prototype requirements and requests for capital purchases come into the department.

The releases from production control will be well systematized whether by some type of electronic system or a manual method – but it's a certainty that the requisitions for consumable items will come in the internal mail, prototype requirements might come in also by internal mail and it is possible that capital purchasing requisitions will be brought to the department by hand.

As these are received in the department, they should all be recorded as received on the day they arrive and perhaps numbered consecutively. The record should contain a brief note as to what is required, who is the requisitioner, by when delivery is required and to which section the requisition has been passed.

The first need for this record is for traceability. If you examine a selection of these requirements as they come into the department, they will fall into several different categories.

1. There will be new requirements for production, demanding the whole process from enquiry to quotation analysis to order. It is probable that if it is a significant item, quote and select will take four weeks. If the order has not been placed in four weeks, it should be reported to you as part of a delinquency report.
2. Schedules for blanket orders are just mailed after the appropriate buyers have checked them quickly to see that they are not impossible to achieve and need not be individually recorded.

3. Requisitions for stores replenishment for nuts, bolts, washers, welding equipment, toilet paper, lubricants, drills, punches, copper hammers etc.

   There should be turned round within two or three days and, if by the end of a seven working-day period there are any not placed, these should be reported to you on a delinquency report.
4. Design prototypes. These can be, say, three shafts machined to a special tolerance, a special bearing, a prototype casting etc.

These are often very difficult to source and Engineering often only find out they need the prototypes the day before they're needed.

The components are often made only by a few suppliers and competitive quoting really is unproductive. Time is the vital element, it is usually a case of inviting the supplier in and getting a quote and a time agreed, face to face.

These should be reported to you as delinquent if the order has not been placed in two weeks.

Anything on the delinquency list should be checked by you.

Probably 'timing to order placing' on the items on the delinquency list should form part of the agenda of your Friday morning management meeting.

If people have genuine hold-ups on the items of the delinquency list, they probably need help and it's up to you to supply the necessary support – even if it's telling the requisitioner that you're not going to be able to meet the required date.

What you are really looking for is any form of slackness or finger trouble. There will be some items that can't meet the customer's lead times – but it's up to the timing process to keep that to the minimum.

After a while, you may want to make a distinction as to the level and category of items that you review in the timing meeting but, at first, you should have all types referred to you.

Part of the benefit of running a timing system based on a delinquency list is that you will see that there are a considerable number of very lazy 'customers' who raise requisitions impossibly late and blame purchasing for their shortage of materials.

This is an education process that you must pay attention to and, until you can improve this situation, there is the need for you to know what is going to be late and why!

Many purchasing managers have become ex-purchasing managers when asked by the engineering director, 'Where is my countershaft order I placed three weeks ago? If I'd have known how long it would take, I would have got it made myself', and replied, 'I don't know'.

Naturally, the engineering director would not ask the purchasing manager for an answer unless it was in front of the MD (the engineering director is going to be late on a test programme and doesn't want the MD to think the blunder is the engineering director's).

If the purchasing manager can reply, 'We received the requisition last week, there are 43 operations required and the supplier is on Op 15 now', the purchasing manager has nothing to fear.

But it means a lot of homework and a good information network within the department to be able to take this stance.

In this chapter it has been made clear how important your policies and procedures are; the timing routine is a procedure of course and the policy which covers it is policy 2, paragraph (h).

You should write up the procedure in detail so that there can be no argument about what you want. Also, the importance and mechanics of budgeting have been highlighted.

One purchasing manager of the writer's acquaintance felt that policies and procedures were a form of bureaucracy until finding out that verbal instructions got quickly forgotten, and then that different buyers and/or different sections were not conforming to company policy. Then the purchasing manager started writing!

It may also seem that the author has showed some distrust about the ethics of Accounts/Finance and Design engineering.

My advice to the purchase manager taking up a first appointment is to prepare for the worst and hope for the best.

7

INVENTORY AND SUPPLY PROTECTION

'Not too much, not too little – but just right.'

One of the responsibilities of Purchasing is that inventory is kept to a minimum, but when coupled with the fact that another responsibility is that production should never be stopped or even inhibited by material shortages, there is a problem of balance to be solved.

This balance is not too difficult to achieve when supplying to a flow-production line, it is more difficult with batch production and more difficult still with 'one-off' production, but it can be done and *is* done all the time by thousands of companies.

It is also very badly done in many more thousands of companies.

Every company which is manufacturing is able to give its buyers four facts:

1. what material is required (specified by design);
2. what quantity is required (specified by production control);
3. when it is required (specified by production control);
4. what quality is required (specified by quality control and design engineering).

From this information, the buyer raises enquiries in which potential suppliers are invited to quote. The buyer also adds, as a minimum, the required date for samples to be submitted and requests also the cost of special tooling etc. that the supplier will require to manufacture and supply the material.

The buyer performs a quotation analysis, selects the best source, raises the order and passes on to the next task. The company that is going to be the most successful in Inventory Control and Supply protection goes much further than this.

Many send out, with the basic enquiry, a set of questions contained in a questionnaire.

There are nine basic questions the supplier must answer and these are also taken into account when the quotation analysis is prepared.

To take a hypothetical case. The buyer enquired for:

> A turned part, made of a particular steel (specified by design) to be delivered at the rate of 100 per day. Starting in three months from the enquiry date. Samples to be provided two months from the enquiry date off production tools.

All the potential suppliers could satisfy volume, dates for samples and production, and each supplied a tool cost. So the buyer's selection was just a simple lowest quote choice.

The nine questions could reveal that the buyer had not selected the supplier who could most satisfactorily provide the lowest ultimate cost.

THE CAPACITY QUESTIONNAIRE

1. What is the hourly rate of the machine you are proposing to employ to manufacture this part?
2. What is the lead time to produce the special tooling required to manufacture this part?
3. Do you have more than one machine that can produce this part?
4. Is the special tooling capable of immediate transfer to this machine?
5. Does the supplier work a single shift or a double shift?
6. What is your lead time for acquisition of raw material?
7. What is your normal transport method for delivering from your works to ours?
8. What is the normal transit time from your works to ours?
9. What is your preferred frequency of delivery to our works?

Although the example we are using refers to a steel-turned component, a similar questionnaire should be employed for all items being bought for production, whether the material is a moulding, casting, forging, pressing, assembly or whatever. Other questions can be added depending on the information that is needed to be obtained in your particular environment.

Analysis of the reply

The reply to each question needs to be analysed carefully.

1. What is the hourly rate of the machine you are proposing to employ to manufacture this part?

The potential suppliers could plan in this case to produce on either a capstan lathe or a multi-spindle automatic lathe. So each could legitimately answer that they could produce 100 per day.

But there's a snag!

The multi-spindle auto could perhaps produce at a rate of 500 per hour, when the capstan might only produce at 20 per hour.

Despite the fact that the enquiry is for a delivery rate of 100 per day, the buyer should also be assured that the supplier has capacity for responding to stock loss replacement, spares orders, unexpected schedule increases, perhaps late rejects etc. and might even sometimes have to double the requirement.

Assuming 40 production hours per week, the most the supplier with a production rate of 20 per hour could produce would be 800 pieces – is this a safe margin from the point of view of manufacture?

This supplier could perhaps only be considered if they answered Question 5 by stating that they double-shift.

This question to the potential suppliers has several other benefits.

(a) The difference in costing the product from a capstan, compared to an auto lies firstly in the difference in the setting-up times of the two machines.

A capstan might only take a few minutes to set up, while setting up the auto could take eight hours. Each machine must earn an hourly rate so while the capstan is chugging on at 20 per hour, the unit cost is high compared to the auto producing 500 per hour. But the unit cost for the items produced off the auto must bear a proportion of the hourly rate when the machine was not earning, i.e. the setting-up time.

So the quotations from the two suppliers might be:

Capstan supplier	£1.00 each
Auto supplier	£0.25 each + SUC £800 (setting up charge)

This should lead the buyer back to the supplier who has quoted using the auto to discuss economic bulk quantity (EBQs).

(b) Economic Bulk Quantity (sometimes also known as Economic Batch Quantity)

Clearly the price of 800 items off the auto would cost £800 (SUC):

800 × 25p = £200 (+ £800 SUC) = £1000

But 800 off the Capstan would cost £800 only.

But, since we require 500 per week indefinitely, it is clear that if we asked the auto supplier to produce and deliver a month's requirement at a time, then off the auto the price becomes:

2000 × 25p = £500 (+ £800 SUC) = £1300

Whereas the cost off the capstan production would be £2000.

2. What is the lead time to produce the special tooling required to manufacture this part?

It could be that both suppliers would require 2 months, but with the supplier with the slower output, if requirements rose above 800 per week – it would be 2 months before output could be stepped up. Even if on a single shift, the supplier decided to put on a night shift, it could take some weeks before new labour could be trained.

Therefore, again the hourly rate affects choice of supplier.

3. Do you have more than one machine that can produce this part?

Probably both suppliers would answer 'Yes'. This guards against a machine breakdown stopping production – provided the answer to Question 4 is also in the affirmative!

(Sometimes suppliers have many machines, but of different manufacture, and adapting the special tooling to another machine can take almost as long as commissioning new tools.)

6. What is your lead time for acquisition of raw material?

Steels, forgings and castings, plastic mouldings etc. can be specified by designers either in simple, easy-to-get raw materials, to the downright difficult to obtain.

If the suppliers both said two to three months, then there is another threat to supply stoppage lurking just below the surface. This can be as great a threat to continuous supply as a tool breakdown or a machine breakdown.

There are a series of actions which the buyer should take at this point:

(a) ask the designers if a more readily obtainable material could be used than the one specified;

(b) decide that the supplier must be given authority to hold material by:
   (i) the schedule always projecting five months out, with authority to procure raw material ahead of the two-month firm requirement
   (ii) to warn the supplier that as a condition of being granted the order, they must always hold three months' stock or raw material etc.

7. What is your normal transport method for delivering from your works to ours?
Probably, the supplier will say, road by carrier or their own transport – but they might say rail, post, air or even sea.

8. What is the normal transit time from your works to ours?
If the material is being sent by road, the supplier may say four hours, for example. In this case, it is advisable to convert this to one day (this is for use in later inventory calculations). They could say that it was post (two days?), air (very quick transit time to your nearest airport), but it can take a couple of days to collect the material from the airport – as well as extra expense. So say two days. And so on.

9. What is your preferred frequency of delivery to our works?
Depending on circumstances, the supplier will say anything from daily, twice weekly, weekly, six monthly, or even that they want the company to collect.

(It will be the cost of the supplier's preferred delivery that will have been worked into the prices. Increase the frequency and the supplier may ask for a price increase, reduce the frequency and you can ask for a price reduction.)

Looking again at the suppliers' quotations in the light of their replies to the questionnaire, then provided you are able to agree with production control that the EBQ choice is the most economical on a once-monthly delivery and that you are able to provide, or agree with the supplier, that they will hold stock of the raw material, then you have a very strong assurance that you have established full supply protection.

Supply protection at minimum inventory

But what does this do to inventory? (NB: 'Borrowing cost' excludes storage cost, loss of working capital etc. and some authorities state that true cost of excess inventory is 36% per annum.)

If, for the moment, we allow the supplier to produce a month's requirement and deliver it, say, every fourth Monday, how much inventory should we be holding when the lorry comes into the receiving bay with the next four weeks' requirement?

We are satisfied that they can produce our normal month's requirement in four hours and that their method of delivery is by their own transport – what can go wrong?

Well . . .

1. The lorry could break down *en route*.
2. The material might arrive and be rejected – although this is a low risk.
3. The supplier may be Scottish – trucks are regularly held up in the winter for several days just north of Carlisle.
4. There is no second source so that tool breakdown could be possible just as the supplier starts the production run.

Pragmatically, the truck breakdown could add one day before a new truck could off-load the broken down one and get material into the plant. Normally, we've stated that we would allow one day for transit. This gives two days.

If the material was rejected, a new consignment could be re-manufactured inside a day and to deliver would take a day, making two days for replacement of rejects.

Thus:

Transit time	1 day
Breakdown and recovery	2 days
Re-manufacture	1 day
Second transit time	1 day

This provides an argument for holding five days' stock when the next delivery arrives.

Thus, normally stock would 'hunt' between five weeks and one week float when the new material arrives.

The 'mean' inventory on this part is 2.5 weeks and assuming that this routine carried on throughout the financial year, the average cost of inventory for this part would be:

65p each × 1250 = £812.50

The borrowing cost for £812.50 @ 15% per annum is £121.87.

If the supplier is prepared to run a month's requirement but deliver weekly, the float remains the same but the inventory 'hunts' between one week and two weeks' stock, thus the 'mean' is 750 pieces at 65p – £325.00 and the borrowing cost becomes £48.75.

As experience grows and confidence grows with the supplier, it could be possible to reduce the float, say, to 2.5 days and perhaps have daily deliveries, so that stock 'hunted' between 2.5 to 3.5 days, which would bring the mean cost of inventory down still further.

It will be clear to the reader that, provided schedules are reliable, stocks can be controlled safely at low stock holdings.

Use of bond stock

When schedules are less reliable, there are still a great many ways open to the buyer to maintain adequate supply and still keep inventory as low as is feasible.

If the production schedules are established using the lead time and float stock holding formula that the buyer has provided – but is still subject to violent swings in terms of time requirement and volume requirement – the creation of a bond stock has an important part to play.

The bond stock is an additional 'float' held at the supplier's charge which is kept in The Company's premises. The supplier maintains normal deliveries and only if they cannot respond to an increased demand does the material in the bond stock get used.

It is a protection to both supplier and customer in that the supplier is not being forced out of a planned production programme in responding to customer panics and the customer has an emergency stock to fall back on. Normally, provided that the customer pays for material taken from bond immediately, the supplier is happy to supply the material and is content not to be paid until the material is used. It is usual to 'purge' the bond stock every six months to avoid deterioration and stock obsolescence, and then recreate the stock.

Once 'bond is broken' the supplier tops up the quantity to the agreed level on the next production run.

Use of buffer stock

Another method to create stock against eventualities is to request the supplier to hold stock on their premises which can be rapidly called off in case of need. The supplier may increase the unit price to cover this investment – but insurance usually costs something.

Where the lead time is caused by the difficulty in obtaining the raw material quickly, the supplier can be empowered to hold raw material in stock on the understanding that if there was found to be no further use for it, the company would compensate the supplier accordingly. This is very often a cheap solution as, normally, there is someone 'out there' looking for the material who will buy it if it is not needed.

There are many ways of classifying the inventory holding target. The capacity questionnaire has a great many uses and is capable of many further refinements. One of the most common is to classify components not only by cost and availability, but also by considering handling, space considerations, value etc.

Operating at minimum stock level

It has already been shown that 20% of the items constitute 80% of the value and equally that 80% of the items only make up 20% of the value.

Since there may only be limited resources available, concentration is focused on the 20% of items.

If, for example, the top item is a casting weighing 250 lb and a usage of 200 per day, it costs £80, and is single sourced.

The objectives are two:

1. lowest feasible inventory holding;
2. supply security.

The casting is loaded after arrival on to a continuous process transfer machinery line and the supplier is 70 miles from The Company. There are motorway connections between the two plants.

By completing a capacity questionnaire, we know the following:

1. hourly rate is 20 castings per hour;
2. lead times for special tooling. Patterns take three months to make but there are always at least two sets available;
3. there are several lines (all identified) on which these castings could be made;
4. patterns can be used on all lines;
5. the supplier works a two-shift system;
6. lead time for raw materials is not a problem as all products produced in this foundry are grey iron and the factory uses a continuous melt process;
7. the normal transport method is by road. The supplier has a fleet of 10-tonne trucks;
8. normal delivery between plants is three hours;
9. delivery as required.

The company's situation

The castings will be machined on a transfer line which can produce on two shifts up to 15 per hour, i.e. 15 × 8 × 2 in 24 hours = 240. But current sales forecast show that only 200 per day will be required and will be machined at the rate of 12.5 per hour.

However, the castings can be produced at the rate of 20 per hour, also on a two-shift system, providing a daily total of 320 if required. Off-loading facilities for the castings can work at a rate of 5 tonnes per hour.

Storage capacity is limited and not to exceed 500 raw castings.

The supplier's preferences

1. The supplier does not want to hold stock and wants to maximize production by working as close to the optimum production level as possible.
2. The supplier wants to clear each day's production daily if possible.
3. The supplier wants to send full loads and not partial loads unless unavoidable (80 castings make a full load).

(These help The Company because the supplier's preferences help to keep unit cost down.)

What is left is a need to reconcile the differences and limitations in order to keep inventory at a safe but low level.

Since off-loading facilities limit intake to 10 tonnes every 2 hours, this means that only 80 castings in every 2 hours can be received. Thus, if the supplier is permitted to deliver 4 vehicles full on Monday (320), Tuesday (320), Wednesday (320) and Thursday (40), they will be able to deliver 12 full loads and 1 half load only.

If all deliveries are made during the day shift, a typical delivery pattern would be:

- Load 1 at 8.00 a.m.
- Load 2 at 10.00 a.m.
- Load 3 at 12.00 noon
- Load 4 at 2.00 p.m.

By Wednesday at 2.00 p.m., 960 would be delivered and 600 would have been machined; leaving a stock of 360 to start Thursday; with 40 more to come.

By the end of Friday night shift, there would be theoretically nil stock left to start Monday morning with.

Since Load 1 would not arrive until 8.00 a.m. on Monday and would take two hours to get to the transfer line, the minimum float that needs to be carried would be the quantity required to cover the first two hours of production. However, prudence would suggest that if the first vehicle broke down, it would be 10.00 a.m. before the next one arrived and a further two hours before that material could get to the transfer line.

Therefore, the float should be:

Start up quantity (first two hours on Monday)	12.5 × 2 = 25
Failure of first vehicle to arrive (second two hours)	12.5 × 2 = 25
Off-loading of second vehicle (two hours)	12.5 × 2 = 25

The float would be 75 and stock would reach (360 + 75) on Wednesday, dwindling back to 75 by Monday morning. It would be prudent to be sure that the foundry's pipeline was so arranged that the vehicle arriving at the company at 8.00 a.m. on Monday could leave the foundry at 5.00 a.m. fully laden.

If the top 20% of items can be controlled in this way, then inventory can be controlled to less than one shift. This requires only good scheduling and good expediting to succeed.

Low value catalogue/consumable items inventory control

With regard to the 80% of items which represent only 20% of value, the indications are that there is at least £3 million of turnover and probably up to £1 million of this group held in inventory.

It is desirable that this inventory is also reduced to the safe minimum – but still preserving supply security.

There is a third objective which becomes more important as the value of the purchases is reduced – and that is another very valuable commodity. Administration! (See Chapter 14.)

If you let it, buying a paperclip can take as long as buying the casting we discussed earlier, and this increases your manning requirements drastically – or you become increasingly burdened with trivia.

Examples where very great savings on the three objectives can be made are:

- stationery;
- standard parts (nuts, bolts, washers, rivets etc.)
- safety clothing;
- paint;
- oil and grease;
- electrical requirements (light fittings, conduits etc.)
- plumbers' requirements (pipe fittings, boiler spares etc.)

- machine shop requirements (drills, cutters, grinding wheels etc.);
- steel bar and sheet.

RATIONALIZATION OF SUPPLY SOURCES

Very often, research will show that your department is flooded with requisitions from various stores areas for quantities of each of these items, and if the requisitioners specify the supplier, you will find that there are many different suppliers being specified for the same or similar component, depending on the requisitioner's preference.

This is causing the company to lose the benefits of bulk purchasing and creating mayhem throughout the supply chain.

In each of the commodity groups, it is possible to establish an annual volume for each of the components that have been requisitioned in the previous 12 months. Then an enquiry should be launched to the suppliers/stockists who have supplied some of the items in the commodity group for *all* of the items in the commodity group.

The reason for launching only to those suppliers who are known to the company is obvious. New potential suppliers should be kept out of this process until the system, which will be established, has existed for at least a year – since there will be learning curve problems to start with.

It will be found that if any of the suppliers see the whole potential that they could supply (if they were found to be the most competitive), every price they will offer will be lower than the prices paid the previous year! Also, the possibility exists to negotiate volume rebates if the volumes you buy exceed pre-set volumes.

So, if a hundred different items were bought from 20 suppliers last year, and each of the suppliers quotes to be the 100% supplier, very good price reductions will accrue.

The quotation analysis in Table 7.1 results from a typical enquiry following this process. It will be seen from the quotation analysis that when some items were being bought from Mumbles, others from Bundles and others yet from Jumbles, at the current prices paid, the annual expenditure on this commodity group would have been £22 955, whereas to buy the total requirement from any of the three suppliers would produce savings.

Comparing the 'bottom lines' gives Mumbles the most attractive quote. But there is a 'sore thumb'. Item CB is more expensive from Mumbles than either of their competitors.

Table 7.1 Quotation analysis

Part number	Current price	Bundles PLC	Mumbles Limited	Jumbles PLC	Estimated annual volume	Bundles PLC	Mumbles Limited	Jumbles PLC	Current
AA	10p ea	9p	7p	11p	20 000	1 800	1 400	2 200	2 000
AB	5p ea	4p	3p	6p	15 000	600	450	900	750
AC	25p ea	26p	22p	24p	900	234	198	216	225
BA	50p ea	45p	30p	50p	11 000	4 950	3 300	5 500	5 500
BB	70p ea	69p	64p	66p	15 000	10 350	9 600	9 900	10 500
BC	10p ea	9p	8p	7p	6 000	540	480	420	600
CA	12p ea	11p	10p	9p	20 000	2 200	2 200	1 800	2 400
CB	11p ea	11p	12p	10p	4 000	440	480	400	440
CC	9p ea	8p	7p	8p	6 000	480	336	480	540
Total cost						21 594	18 444	22 296	22 955

Saving = £4511 (19.65%)

If Mumbles were to supply at the level of either of the prices offered by the competition, you would save between £40 to £80 per annum more, so they should be requested to reduce their price on this item.

It is probable that these items are held in stores under a stock-holding and inventory control system which depends on a 'float' of 30 days' inventory when the next delivery is made.

The inventory value is likely to be around £1833 per month on this set of items.

Administration savings on catalogue/low value consumable items

If you were to then suggest to Mumbles that they controlled your inventory by a visit, stockcheck and weekly top-up using only, say, two days of stock at the end of each week, you could cut your inventory carrying cost from (as it were) a permanent loan from the bank of £1833, to effectively no loan at all, because if you are paying your supplier only at 30 days, your only outgoing is the cost of materials delivered in the past 30 days.

You would then create a blanket order which lists all the items on the quotation analysis and agree a fixed price for a year.

The benefits from this are as follows.

1. When small orders to companies like Mumbles are placed, the price they offer is out of their catalogue and is subject to price breaks, i.e. 5 to 50 components £1.00 each, 51 to 100 £0.95 each, 101 to 250 £0.93 each. Every so often, they revise all their prices (upwards) and you start to pay a new price. You can be quite certain that all three suppliers would have increased their prices during the coming year.
2. Given that you have created the order and prices are fixed, then stores can handle the stocking with Mumbles, and no requisitions have to be raised at all.
3. If other materials are required which Mumbles can supply, then they should be asked to quote, and the new part and price added to the blanket order by a purchasing order amendment, and the stores list updated by the addition of the new information.
4. The buyer should ensure that the supplier invoices monthly the material they have delivered and checks the invoice to ensure that stores have controlled inventory, i.e. that the supplier has not over-delivered.
5. Hundreds of requisitions no longer have to be raised (saving in Purchasing's process time).
6. One negotiation per annum only instead of a telephone call and discussion for each requisition. (Purchasing can do a 'set-piece' negotiation instead of many *ad hoc* telephone calls.)
7. A purchasing saving of £4511 per annum (19%), a saving of inventory cost of the interest on a loan of £1833 (inventory value) and if the requisitions were all raised by one stores department member, that person can do more production stores work.
8. Supplier portfolio reduced by two, producing another administration saving.

This is a very standard general-purpose technique which can be applied to many, if not all, 'non-production items'.

The buyers' customers have to be satisfied that the new supplier can provide just as good a commodity as whoever was their favourite source, and this requires some PR work – but very few managers will argue against a profit improvement project.

So, provided you can show a good saving with improved service, and a product at least as good as they formerly received, then the NIMBYs can be persuaded to accept your guidance.

Buying based on last year's usage as forecast requirement

The reader may want to ask, 'What happens if the forecast I provided (probably last year's consumption figures) varies in the current order?'

The supplier is basically orientated to 'making money' and if, because of swings in requirement you end up buying a different 'mix' than the original forecast supposed, provided they are making the turnover/profit level they were aiming at, they won't be at all bothered.

If, by chance, your total turnover is down across all the items this will not become an issue between you until the end of the first year. It may then be that they want to increase their price for the following year to compensate for their expectations not being realized.

You have the initiative if you care to use it to put out enquiries on lower volumes for the following year, and if they are market competitive, you renew the current supplier's blanket order, if not, place the order elsewhere, where and if they are more competitive.

The writer's experience is, however, that suppliers in the main don't want to lose business, so that they are always open to proposals from the buyer and, when they have a good order, they will compete hard to keep the business.

Testing the market

By putting the items on each blanket order out on enquiry annually, you are testing the market and now can feed new suppliers into the equation, who may be able to help you achieve your objectives by making suggestions you have not thought of.

The study obtained from finance showed £3 000 000 being spent on consumables and a further £2 000 000 on standard parts, so there is at least £5 000 000 where these techniques are nearly always applicable (in part, even if not completely). There is a potential 20% of turnover open to be saved and a reduction of suppliers of unknown proportions to boot!

Your bar steel purchases, paint and copper will be open also to blanket order competitive enquiry and getting various simplified methods of placing factory requirements with the supplier in place can also be arranged, thus further reducing the flood of requisitions and reducing the number of suppliers on the books.

It will be seen that inventory can be reduced in many ways as you work your way towards 'not too much, not too little – but just right'.

JIT

For inventory to be 100% right is when no material at all is being held in inventory. This, of course, is JIT (just in time).

Over the last decade, there has been much discussion about the cleverness of the Japanese in their application of JIT as though it was their invention.

It was being used in some areas of the motor industry to the writer's certain knowledge during the 1950s, when the only transit time allowed was 2 hours, when there were two 8-hour shifts to be supplied in every 24 hours.

The process was that each 5 days' schedule was produced based on the actual cars that were to be built and in which hour of the 16 hours on each day the specific car was to be built. This meant that the expeditor and the supplier always knew for the next five days that, say, on a Monday during hour number three, the following seats, squabs etc. would be required.

There were many hundreds of different permutations.

First, there were the colour trims, then the type of car, the bench seat or bucket seat and then the covering material, so that the planning of the schedule, once established, could not be changed. That meant that on Monday at hour three to four, there would be: '50 light car rear seats without armrest, 6 red, 4 blue, 20 grey, etc. 100 light car front seats. Left-hand drive, 4 red, 2 blue, 10 grey, and right-hand drive, 2 red, 2 blue, 10 grey and so on through medium cars, heavy cars, trucks and vans.'

The method was that the five-day schedule was telexed to the supplier on every fourth day so the supplier always knew what was required for today, five days in advance.

As each railway container was loaded by the supplier, the company received a telex saying that in rail container XYZ 350 were hour three to four seats. It only remained for the expediter to call into the factory container XYZ 350 from the rail-head at the end of hour two.

Provided the schedule can be produced this accurately, JIT is easy.

All the methods discussed in this chapter work well and, as they are implemented, inventory is reduced and supply protection ensures production continuity.

A word of caution

During the 1970s when it was not unusual to have up to 20% of suppliers on strike at the same time, buyers and production controllers were making their desired inventory calculations based on the fact that the average strike took seven working days. So the aim was to try to obtain enough material to stand-off the normal supplier strike!

Perhaps those years have passed away, never to return – but it is worthwhile to keep an eye on your suppliers' labour relations – because you never know!

8
THE SUPPLIER – FRIEND OR FOE?

There was a sales director of a very famous company supplying extensively to the electronics industry who used to present a normal visiting card giving his name, company, telephone number etc., and in the bottom right-hand corner were the letters 'PTO'. The back of the card, slightly bowlderized, read as follows:

> At the moment, it is a Buyers' Market, hence I'm around every day kissing your foot. When it becomes a Sellers' Market again, I shall be on the golf course and unobtainable to buyers, and then you can kiss *my* foot!

At the same time, there was another famous character, the purchasing manager of a most prestigious company, who used to refer to all suppliers as 'fair weather friends'. He would march majestically through the purchasing office, stop at the desk of a junior buyer up to his neck in crocodiles and boom at him, 'And how many fair weather friends have you hit for six today?' 'Hitting a fair weather friend for six' was achieving a price reduction!

Both men have long since retired, laden with the laurels of many years' faithful service to their respective companies.

To see those two locked in titanic struggle negotiating prices was like watching two champion wrestlers, each seeking a moment's advantage to pin the other down. Yet they had great respect for each other as worthy opponents, and when one needed help in a supply matter, or the other needed a bad price correcting, they each helped the other.

Purchasing since their hey-day has changed greatly, but still the buyers and suppliers struggle for advantage: the methods and tools can be much more sophisticated but the contest remains the same.

The buyer wants the best price possible and the supplier wants the best price possible, but the trouble is that there's 10% or 15% difference in the two people's definition of best price!

The typical supplier who makes and sells a product has the prime objective of making profit. The methods of doing this are composed of a series of sub-objectives which form the supplier's strategy.

THE SUPPLIER'S STRATEGY

1. To be able to compete successfully against the competition. (This is the real yardstick because buyers encourage competition.)
2. To stay competitive they must specialize in certain product ranges where they can concentrate on tooling, capital equipment, design and quality.
3. To consider the possibility of taking work on at cost to pay the overhead while seeking other work on which they can make a considerable profit.
4. To target companies who will buy their product at a suitable price to them.
5. To go out for big volumes. (Benefits of repetition.)
6. To go out for big accounts. (Giving them 'clout' with a customer.)
7. Not to reveal more than is strictly necessary about company details – this gives the buyer a possible advantage in negotiation.
8. To balance the big account with the need to diversify across a range of industries so that if defence is going down, their sales in the chemical industry will keep them solvent.
9. To maintain a good reputation in the market place.
10. To find customers who are good payers – but not very good organizers or co-ordinators. It gives the suppliers' salespeople the opportunity to manipulate a poorly co-ordinated company to their own ends.

Each of the 10 supplier's objectives are also the objectives of the sales organization of the company – but somewhat opposed to the buyer's objectives of lowest ultimate cost! Thus, the supplier's sales personnel must devise tactics to support their strategy, namely the supplier's sales techniques.

SUPPLIER'S SALES TECHNIQUES

There are at least four different types of supplier and their tactics vary according to their type of business:

1. proprietary item suppliers;
2. capital equipment suppliers;
3. consumable items;
4. make to order.

Proprietary item suppliers

A proprietary item is one which is made and marketed to specialist customers. A purely hypothetical product – an hydraulic pump is made and marketed by Bumble-B PLC and the sales director is Abraham McTavish.

Because he keeps close contact with the design team of the company and because he discusses knotty problems with them and helps them with their hydraulics problems, they only think of Bumble-B PLC when they want development work done.

It's McTavish's aim to avoid the buyer entirely while he is persuading the designers to give him development work. He will often say, 'Well your buyers are very good at buying pens and toilet paper, but we engineers understand each other and the buyers are so untechnical that they just inhibit the dialogue we can have between us'.

He buys the designers a few lunches and, very soon, these trusting people have awarded him a design contract. Since they have a budget for this development of £12 000 (which they have *told* him they have), it just so happens that to do the development work will cost just £11 000. The engineers raise the requisition, accept the Bumble-B standard form of contract and ask Purchasing to raise a confirming order. The engineers are *so* pleased that they've saved £1000 of their budget. (It could have been had for nothing because the development costs are recovered in unit price!) McTavish knows too that provided his development work is technically satisfactory, the designers will specify his hydraulic pump for production and Purchasing cannot even offer up competition because Bumble-B PLC will patent and copyright the design.

Purchasing may be allowed to chip £1 or £2 off the price for production volumes but that's all.

If Purchasing want to resource they must find a supplier who can circumvent the Bumble-B patent and get design engineering to test the competitor's product. Naturally, they are very unwilling to admit that they could have chosen a better source if they'd consulted Purchasing first. So they throw every objection into the way of their having to re-test a competitor's product.

By developing the 'inside track', the McTavishs of this world ensure that their product gets approved status before the buyers find out what's going on and, by that time, it's too late.

The wise purchasing manager who is aware that this goes on takes the following precautions.

1. The purchasing manager insists that no development contract is to be placed until purchasing has ensured that at least three companies in the appropriate field have been asked to quote to carry out the development.

   The designers who spend a lot of their time trying to 'pump' suppliers to implement their own ideas feel that purchasing are trying to cut them off from the 'state of the art' information in the market and they will try to frustrate this move.
2. Any supplier who obtains a development contract must agree that the intellectual property of the development remains the company's.
3. Development contracts are awarded on a time and materials basis, and the time and materials deployed are checked weekly by purchasing.
4. This is an area where the purchasing manager must be vigilant and may include having to insist with all suppliers that they do not visit design engineering, except in the company of a buyer.

Capital equipment suppliers

Capital equipment can be anything from machine tools to building projects. The McTavishs in the machine tool industry play in exactly the same way as their colleagues in the proprietary items group, except that their target is the production engineering group.

Their ploy is to persuade the production engineers to believe their machine is the best for a particular purpose. They then provide the production engineers with their specification.

The production engineers then have the spec retyped and issue it to the three suppliers who make the same types of machine, but which may have some different features.

Clearly the only supplier who can exactly meet the spec is the one whose machine the spec was written around in the first place.

(It is not that unusual to find a production engineer so bewitched by a few dinners and a couple of visits to a football match that they will move heaven and earth to get their favourite supplier's machine accepted.)

Normally, the production engineer will say, 'It's the best – and we must pay for quality!'

Getting capital machinery buying into a situation where potential suppliers are playing on a flat field is a very time-consuming business, but it is very rewarding in cost terms.

Production engineers are often members of fairly militant trade unions and they will even try to get their union to keep out Purchasing on the basis that they are engineers and should not be interfered with by a non-technical arm. The writer has seen over the years strikes and work to rule action by production engineers in defence of their patch.

Eventually, however, they are persuaded to write neutral specs which define the operations that they require, speeds and feeds etc., and the spec can be sent out by Purchasing to the appropriate number of potential sources.

When the quotes are returned, the buyer, together with the production engineer, can make an analysis of the different features offered.

A feature analysis

The purpose is to establish a level playing field between competing suppliers. A simple example could be in the comparison you might make between three cars:

	Car A	Car B	Car C
Engine	1500 cc	1500 cc	1500 cc
Fuel	Petrol	Petrol	Petrol
Seats	Plastic	Leather	Mock leopard skin
Window operation	Manual	Electric	Electric
Max speed	100 m.p.h.	150 m.p.h.	90 m.p.h.
External trim	None	Plastic	Chrome steel
Wheels	Plain	Sculptured	Sculptured
	£8000	£9000	£9500

If the specification was for a standard representative's car capable of 70 m.p.h. only – then A is the right choice.

The features cost an extra £1000 for Car B and £1500 for Car C for no apparent benefit.

Very often, the production engineer will feel that Car B has got all these special features on it which make it more desirable, and will opt for B.

Often when asked, 'Do you really think that leather trim, electric windows, sculptured wheels and a maximum speed of 150 m.p.h. justify an extra £1000?, they start to get the point.

Machine tool suppliers often build on features as unnecessary to the function of the machine as where electrically opened windows are added to a car in order to build up the cost of their machines.

In truth, the difference between the price of Car A and Car B at works cost level is unlikely to be more than £50 – but it helps marketing to increase the margin.

If the engineer did want a feature the equivalent of the leather trim, then it should be paid for – but the other bits are not wanted and shouldn't be included in the adjusted quote. It is only when the suppliers are quoting on a like for like basis that their quotes can be adjusted to a common base and a price negotiation commenced.

Building projects

Probably worse than the sales techniques of the McTavishs who set out to control design engineers and production engineers are those of the local builders, surveyors and architects who play golf with the MD.

The typical scenario is that at the monthly board meeting, the need for extra covered space is identified. It may be in the shape of new offices or new production facilities.

The board member who is proposing the new facility is doubtless expanding his or her empire. Nobody else on the board (unless there is a purchasing director also on the board) will ask if the proposer has looked at buying out the extra production rather than committing to a new building and new labour, or improving systems within the existing office space to avoid the necessity of the extra expenditure.

Instead, the board with no purchasing representative are immediately off on to dreams of a building taller than the Empire State building and bigger in area than Euston railway station.

The minute in the board meeting report will read:

> New building
> The MD instructed the facilities director to produce for the next board meeting a sketch of the proposed location of the building and some ideas as to its construction etc.

The MD, at this stage, decides to talk to some cronies at the golf club.

At the 19th hole after a couple of stiff G&Ts, the MD says to one of the partners of a local firm of architects, 'Why don't you pop in to see me during the week and I'll introduce you to my facilities director.'

The meeting takes place. The next thing that anybody knows is that the architects are now designing the new building with a contract. The facilities director didn't want to waste an engineer's time on the job anyhow.

Two board meetings later, the architects produce some interesting drawings showing nicely coloured elevation drawings beautifully screened with stands of trees and the board all make approving noises. The architects also are praising the skills of Bloggs & Bloggs who are their favourite builders, such good work, so economical etc.

Then the MD asks the Purchasing Manager to raise an order to pay the architects their fee and to raise an order on Bloggs & Bloggs for the building. The architects have also elected themselves as main contractor so that they will negotiate with the plasterers, carpenters, electricians, plumbers etc. on a 'price to be agreed' basis.

When the contract starts to go wrong and all the hidden costs come to light, the board ask, 'Who signed the orders to allow this incredible blunder to take place?'

New purchasing managers can very rapidly become ex-purchasing managers in this scenario.

There should always be purchasing representatives at board level and when there are not, the Purchasing Manager must insist on investigating the whole arrangement at the time of being asked by the MD to place the orders on the builders and pay the architects.

Chapter 12 will explain in detail what should take place.

Consumable items

Although we have seen some examples of 'amateur buyers' from board level through design and facilities engineers, they are at least relatively small in numbers.

In the area of consumables in an average-sized company there are hundreds of 'amateur buyers'.

Stationery

All the secretaries want different word processors, their bosses want their own style of stationery and insist on requisitioning these odd requirements.

Very often, because stationery representatives are visiting the secretaries they are *selling* to them.

Laboratory equipment

The lab is another fertile ground for representation from stockists. Each lab technician wants a balance supplied by a different company than that of a colleague, and wants to specify the agent from whom glassware is to be bought etc.

If the lab technicians have their own budget, and many have, they feel they must spend every penny each year because if they don't, they won't have the same allowance next year.

Thus no compunction is felt about ordering the most expensive gear – even if it is not needed in order to preserve the budget proportion.

Drills, grinding wheels, lubricants, cutters, measuring equipment etc.

Stockists' representatives persuade foremen and superintendents that Snibbo's products are better than anyone else's and so they always requisition Snibbo, except for their colleagues who have been conversely persuaded that Dingo equipment is the best.

Make to order suppliers

In many companies, if the business methods of quotation, quote analysis and select are properly in place, this area is reasonably under control but even here, unscrupulous buyers have been known to place their enquiries to two suppliers who will return no quotes and, the third quote being the only one received, gets the order. The 'successful' supplier was the one the buyer wanted. The other two companies don't make the product the buyer was enquiring for.

THE PURCHASING MANAGER AS WATCHDOG

This chapter is entitled 'Supplier – Friend or Foe?'. From the foregoing, it is plain that suppliers will use the weaknesses and fallibilities of their customers in order to achieve profit, and they shouldn't be blamed for doing this, any more than a watchdog should be blamed for biting an intruder.

Nevertheless, the new Purchasing Manager has been given the role of watchdog and must show to the supplier community that they don't bark very much but they do have a fearsome bite!

In order to get into the position of being able to ensure that all items bought, big or small, are subjected to competitive study and that the lowest ultimate costs are the sole criteria, the purchasing manager has to set up several 'early-warning systems'.

In Chapter 1, accounting provided a list of all the suppliers used in the past 12 months and how much they were paid.

Analysis will show that, perhaps, there were 10 suppliers used for the same commodity in this area, 12 in another commodity area and so on.

Using the method of quotation analysis described in Chapter 7, it is feasible to select one supplier to cover all requirements.

The next step is to advise each of the requisitioners who were buying from their own pet supplier of the benefits of a single approved source. The argument that purchasing have to use is quite straightforward:

1. lowest ultimate cost;
2. saving time for the other disciplines to spend more time on their own jobs.

So, you must watch the requisitions as they come into the department to see that they are following the agreement that has been made.

But the salespeople for the competitors, although knowing that for the moment they have lost the business, will still come in and try to persuade the users that, 'Purchasing don't know what they're doing etc. You have a perfect right to spend your budget as you please etc'.

Discontent may smoulder and, unless you move quickly, will burst into open disobedience. This is normal in the writer's experience because the 'amateur buyers' feel that their wings have been clipped.

One precaution that should be taken is that you should arrange with Security that any representatives who call at the factory should be directed to Purchasing and *no one else*, until the reason for their visit is explained. Then it is up to Purchasing if they go on to their planned meeting or the business they came to transact is conducted in the Purchasing offices.

While in Chapter 6 some of the disadvantages of budgetary control were aired, an alliance between Accounting and Purchasing can be profitable to the company if the following early warning system is instigated.

No matter how good at foreseeing the future the average 'budgeter' is, there are special needs which arise during the year. Often these are in the area of capital requirements. A large sum may be set aside, and from this sum, monies are requisitioned in two stages.

First, a project is raised and a sum estimated for the project and, subsequently, after board approval for the project, monies are drawn down for each leg of the project.

Accounting can provide a copy of the original project to Purchasing – who may not have been involved, although they should have been. Clearly, Purchasing have the duty to submit to the board their view and, since each subsequent tranche of money required also has to be approved, the Purchasing manager is able to see what is being requested and can 'state his or her case' prior to the deployment of the next expenditure.

It may be that in the drive to control the 'spenders', you will find totally unreasonable choices of suppliers which keep occurring despite the procedures that you are putting into place.

Here you must suspect that there is fraud taking place.

You may find that the production engineer who always specifies Zulu-Alpha grinding machines is a director of Zulu-Alpha – or that his wife is, or that Mrs M, the secretary of the personnel director, is the wife of the sales manager of Tango-Foxtrot stockists.

Or, again, Mr Bloggs the foreman of the assembly shop has had a new kitchen installed by the supplier who he always specified for jigs and fixtures.

These suppliers are your foes who you must root out and, while it's difficult to prove, the company employees go too.

In a later chapter, the business of cost control and negotiation will be discussed together with the aim of building a partnership with suppliers via the cost control negotiation processes.

One final thing, no matter how businesslike and friendly your relationships become, remember two things.

1. The supplier's best price and your best price are 10% to 15% apart, always!
2. Never be fooled by the 'good relationship'. The day you are no longer 'the one with the power' you will be forgotten and 'a new one with the power' will inherit your robes.

9

SUPPLIER EVALUATION METHODS, COST ESTIMATION AND PRODUCT COST CONTROL

In Chapter 8, the strategies employed by some suppliers were discussed and some more or less standard penetration techniques were identified, where some potential suppliers will attempt to exploit weaknesses in the company's organization in order to compel purchasing to buy their product.

PURCHASING INITIATIVES IN SOURCE SELECTION

Purchasing should always hold the initiative in source selection – in other words, *purchasing* make the choices – not the amateur buyers acting misguidedly under the control of certain suppliers.

There are plenty of suppliers in all fields who have:

1. a good financial base;
2. a good production facility;
3. a good quality control system;
4. a good management team;
5. a professional and ethical sales force;
6. a competitive pricing policy;
7. a flexible delivery and manufacturing process.

However, many suppliers that you can encounter every day do not match these standards; and it is very easy to select one of them as a supplier and then rue the day thereafter. Until you have the benefit of a group of approved suppliers around you to choose from, who do meet your requirements, this is a constant danger.

In Chapter 1 it was made clear that there were a number of current suppliers who were not providing 100% quality performance, others who were failing to achieve 100% on delivery performance, while yet others were apparently not market competitive on price.

From the reports from quality control showing batches received and batches rejected, and late deliveries reported by production control, you should very quickly be able to build up a dossier on your current suppliers, showing the following.

SUPPLIER PERFORMANCE REPORT

Week Commencing	30/9	7/10	14/10	21/10	28/10	4/11	11/11	18/11	25/11
Able Ltd									
Batches rec	5	7	6	9	4	8	6	5	9
Batches rej		2		3	1	1	–	–	3
Deliveries scheduled	10	14	14	14	14	15	15	15	15
Deliveries late	1	–	–	3		2	–	–	2
Cum perf quality %		16.0%	11.0%	18.5%	19.3%	17.9%	15.5%	14%	
Cum delivery performance	10%	4.1%	2.6%	7.6%	6.0%	7.4%	6.2%		

Over this period, it will be seen that Able on quality performance by batch are only getting 86% cumulatively past inspection and deliveries of the batches (some partial deliveries) are cumulatively only achieving 93.8% accuracy.

In order to complete the picture, it is advisable to establish a similar view of the following.

1. Supply flexibility, i.e. ability to change at short notice from production of an item which had been scheduled to production of a panic. (Some of Able's problems could have been caused by attempting to respond to panics.)
2. Willingness of supplier to negotiate on price which should include:
   (a) willingness to show operation sheets;
   (b) willingness to conduct 'open-book' negotiations;
   (c) competitiveness.
3. Financial standing (of suppliers)
   (If suppliers go bankrupt, supply is very often in extreme jeopardy.)

   Sections 1 and 2 require reports from the people in regular contact with the supplier and a score out of 10 possible marks, although slightly subjective, is in fact a reliable guide since the people scoring the supplier know what level of service and co-operation they receive.

   The financial standing of a supplier is valuable information, both in negotiation and in the day-to-day dealings with the supplier, and every effort should be made to establish a view of their situation.

   Methods available to assess
   (a) Suppliers should be requested to provide copies of their annual reports – many do this automatically but some do not – unless they are asked!
   (b) Dun and Bradstreet reports. This company provides reports on a range of aspects which provide indicators to a company's financial health. An annual subscription is required in order to enjoy Dun and Bradstreet's services.
   (c) Stockbrokers' year book.
   (d) Day-to-day reports in the *Financial Times* and other newspapers.
   (e) Reference to other buyers in your industry.
   (f) Industry commentaries.

It will be seen that all of the above will provide useful indicators – although none, of course, will provide a full picture. The suppliers' annual reports are as glossy as possible and have been presented by the accountant in such a way as to disguise any unpleasantness. They have also been audited by a respectable company of auditors, which should give confidence.

However, auditors have been known to certify an account only a week or two before the supplier goes bankrupt!

SUPPLIERS' ANNUAL REPORTS

Nevertheless, suppliers' annual reports provide valuable information, if analysed as below.

(a) Total sales

The question to ask is 'What is the percentage of the company's spend with this supplier?'

This is to check your exposure with the supplier. Clearly, if your spend represented, say, 30% of total sales, you would be a most important customer, but you might consider yourself too much in their hands for safety. On the other hand, if your business dropped off with the supplier – could they survive?

This latter *is* a concern of yours because of the bad press you could get if your decision to resource did, in fact, cause the closure of the supplier.

(b) Profit before tax

By expressing this figure as a percentage of total sales, you can deduce what percentage profit the supplier may be making on sales to you!

A buyer expects suppliers to make profit – because otherwise, the buyer has got a supplier who may fold up at any time – but what is a fair profit? Is it fair that despite the fact that the supplier is most competitive, they are making a bigger percentage profit than you are? After all, the further down the supply chain you are from the raw material, the greater the risk.

(c) Inventory

By comparing total sales with inventory, it is possible to deduce the times-turn of inventory and gain a view of the efficiency of the company.

High inventory usually indicates slackness from at least two viewpoints.

- Financial sloth and high unnecessary borrowings.
- Poor stock control because, invariably, high inventory is made up of slow-moving stock (or even dead stock not written off) which can often mean that the supplier, in order to keep the stock figure within bounds, controls live requirements very tightly – and this may put your requirements on to shortage, which can put your job in jeopardy.

(d) Number of employees

The number of employees in the organization will, over a few years, show a trend – it may be up or down. Either way, this is of interest to you and you should find out why this is occurring.

If the number of employees is expressed as a ratio to total sales, a good yardstick exists to see how efficient the company is in thousands of pounds earned per employee per annum.

(e) Total current assets

Debtors, inventory, bank balance and investments: this group of assets are established at a point in time and should be compared, *less* inventory with total current liabilities.

(f) Total current liabilities

Creditors, bank overdrafts, outstanding taxes, dividends etc.: this provides a view of their ability to meet current liabilities.

If at the same time, you take out a Dun and Bradstreet report on this supplier, it will tell you:

- whether there have been any judgments against the supplier for non-payment of debts;
- the credit that this supplier is allowed by suppliers etc.

You will now have a view of the supplier's financial health and some ammunition for future negotiations. One point to remember, however, is that in periods of recession, compared to periods of boom, the number of suppliers sailing very close to the wind is very high and you can still get some nasty surprises.

Often your award of business can mean the difference between success and failure for your suppliers. You must demand the highest levels of performance from your suppliers, therefore, you too may have to take some decisions which could result in pushing the less efficient suppliers over the edge.

Up until now in this chapter, we have been quantifying our existing suppliers – now we will move into new supplier research.

NEW POTENTIAL SUPPLIERS – RESEARCH METHODS

1. Trade journals.
2. Sales representatives calling.
3. Exhibitions.
4. Competitors' products.
5. Buyers' guides (*Kompass*, *Kellys*, *Engineering*, *Electronics* etc.).
6. Enquiries to embassies and consulates.
7. *BSI Buyers' Guide*.

Each of the above routes are very productive sources of information, but the use that the researching buyer puts them to differs according to need. Time has to be set aside daily or weekly to read appropriate trade journals where suppliers to the industry will be discussing their products.

If their products are those in which you are interested, then a set of enquiries should be sent to the potential source. Similarly, if there are industry exhibitions at which products are being shown that are of interest, enquiries should be placed with the appropriate exhibitors.

No buyers should ever be put in the position where they can say, 'I'm too busy to read journals or visit exhibitions' – it's part of their job!

As quotations are received back from these potential sources, the buyer will gain a view of their price structure and, normally, will also receive brochures of the supplier's company and perhaps – and always useful – a plant list defining their equipment in order to help the buyer start to formulate a review.

The buyer should remember that the prices offered could be different to the price expected – this can be due to the supplier 'firing blind' and hoping to meet the buyer face to face to talk about the company's requirements or it may be a true indication of the pricing structure.

Some of the more advanced purchasing organizations send with their enquiries to potential suppliers a booklet which describes the way in which they do business to help the new supplier to quote more precisely and you may wish to produce such a booklet yourself to fulfil this need.

While most of the suppliers in northern Europe, the US, Canada and Japan tend to quote a price which they believe to be attractive to the buyer and demonstrates *their* pricing policy – although still open to negotiation – this is not the case in other countries.

In Italy, for example, the usual technique is to quote high with the aim of provoking a face-to-face negotiation. Unfortunately, many UK buyers not realizing this, tend to throw the quote away as being too dear – and a good opportunity is wasted.

In India, the tendency is to attempt to find out the world price and quote that. Like the Italians, they lose business because the UK buyer has the tendency to 'junk' any quotation that does not immediately present a lower price than the current price.

If the buyer decides to take the matter further, the next task is to visit the supplier and carry out an audit. In most companies, this first audit is called the commercial audit, and if the buyer is impressed as a result of this audit, a quality audit and perhaps a production engineering audit as well will be called for.

The commercial audit

This should take the form of a standardized questionnaire which should include the following questions.

By completion of this questionnaire on each commercial audit undertaken, the knowledge of the relative abilities and capabilities of suppliers grows and, with it, selection of sources by these factors gradually replaces the shotgun enquiry system – so that enquiries are only placed with *selected* sources who have a known capability to produce the requirement efficiently.

If, after such an audit, the buyer wants to recommend a quality audit in which the potential supplier's quality methods are checked out in detail, the buyer has obviously been satisfied with their commercial abilities.

It may be that the Quality Control (QC) report may say that there are certain areas which must be improved prior to QC accepting the potential supplier as an approved source.

In this case, the potential supplier should be advised to rectify the complaints and then allow QC to return to satisfy themselves that the complaints have been dealt with.

THE APPROVED SUPPLIER'S CONTRACT

It might be advisable to ask production engineering to inspect the potential supplier's production facilities – depending on the type of product and given then that they are satisfied, the way lies open to

COMMERCIAL AUDIT	
1. Supplier name and address	Telephone number Fax Telex
2. Company structure	Plc Privately owned etc.
3. Management structure and names	Chairperson Managing director Sales director Engineering director Purchasing director
4. Number of factories and location	Brief description:
5. Associations with other companies	Ownership Sister companies
6. Founded	History:
7. Factory: (a) Area of plant (b) Extension opportunity (c) Structure (d) Ownership, i.e. rented?	 (a) (b) (c) (d)
8. Conditions of buildings	Brief description
9. Employees	Staff Hourly paid
10. Processes carried out: (a) State: Capacities (b) Obtain plant list (c) Facilities	 (a) (b) (c)
11. Major customers <2% Of supplier's turnover	
12. Quality control approvals AQUAP, BS5750 etc.	

Commercial Audit *continued*

13. Wage review anniversaries	
14. Industrial relations history	
15. Financial status (balance sheet) Do they accept material labour and overhead costing?	
16. Prepared to hold stocks?	
17. Payment terms	
18. Carriers Own transport? Other?	
19. Toolmakers Own Other	
20. Internal scheduling system	
21. Internal purchasing resources	

negotiate an Approved Supplier Contract with the potential supplier *even before a single order has been placed.*

The contract signed with an Approved Source should contain the following seven basic clauses.

1. The supplier agrees to accept the buyer's terms and conditions.
2. The supplier agrees to warrant all items to be in line with all specifications, drawings etc., as furnished by the company and to supply the company as a quality assured company.
3. The supplier agrees to hold, at their charge, mutually agreed safety stocks.
4. The supplier agrees to negotiate on the basis of material, labour and overhead costs, and to maintain a method of 'open-book' price negotiations and maintain world-competitive prices.
5. The supplier agrees to inform the buyer as early as possible in any or each of the following cases:

(a) apparent likelihood of not meeting a delivery date;
(b) apparent likelihood of industrial relations problems impingeing on production plans;
(c) possible cost reduction which could be obtained by improved manufacturing methods;
(d) possible cost reductions obtainable by design changes.

6. In return, the buyer will ensure that enquiries for all items which are perceived to be within the potential supplier's range will be offered to the supplier.
7. The buyer will undertake to advise the supplier where they are being challenged by prices offered by competition and give them the opportunity to reconsider their prices prior to undertaking resourcing action.

Others can be added, such as, when Design are considering a new design, the supplier may be invited to assist the engineers in resolving their design difficulties etc.

Termination of such a contract, if deemed necessary, should state:

> If either party is not performing to the letter and spirit, the other can terminate after say three months. This three months, or whatever period is chosen, is to provide the buyer time to resource should the contract fail to be productive at any time, and should relate to the tooling and launch time that would be required.

This contract can be modified to cover special requirements and suppliers who become 'approved' are normally very pleased to have achieved this position and are willing to go that 'extra mile' when The Company request it.

Ideally, there should not be more than three or four Approved Suppliers per commodity range in operation at any given time.

New potential suppliers can be allowed Approved status – but they should *replace* an existing source since increasing the number of Approved Sources leads to proliferation of suppliers and reduction of turnover lodged with each supplier.

Each Approved Supplier's items should be put out on enquiry on an annual basis to the market in general and their prices tested against those available in the world market – it is, however, not unusual to find that some Approved Sources become so much a part of The Company that they remain the most competitive indefinitely.

From the foregoing, it will be seen that it is possible to be able to evaluate suppliers to ensure success in finding the best supply sources. Most importantly, it is the *buyer* who establishes the sources that the company will use, not the sharp salesrep., or the amateur buyer!

COST ESTIMATION

As the subject of material, labour and overhead have been touched upon in various aspects of deciding cost, and the approved supplier contract requests that this method of costing is utilized to determine price, it is often worth while to have the use of estimators. These are production-engineering trained people who are able to envisage the way a component should be made and estimate the minutes of labour required to produce the part, off a certain type of machinery or manufacturing system.

Some Purchasing departments establish a group of production engineers within Purchasing – others obtain assistance from the Production Engineering department, a large percentage of buyers have also developed this skill.

A simply estimate for a pressing might only require, say, three operations:

1. blank;
2. pierce;
3. form.

The blanking operation cuts out the developed blank from a sheet or strip, the second punches the holes required in the finished item and the third operation bends the pressing to the appropriate shape.

The estimator would envisage this production process from the drawing and would also envisage the type of press and the tooling required to produce this item at the lowest ultimate cost.

PREPARATION OF THE ESTIMATE

Starting with the raw material, it is possible to buy steel in sheet at a standard size or buy it in strip form.

If it is bought in standard sheet size and can be blanked from the sheet, it is cheaper than buying the strip from the stockist. It may be that the supplier's presses have to feed in strip form, in which case the supplier may be able to convert the sheet they buy to strip form by use of their own equipment, rather than buy the steel in strip form.

Thus, the estimator can decide, by considering the tooling, the size of the component and the quantity required, the most economical way to buy the steel.

The three operations, blank, pierce and form, can be done on three separate presses, with handling between each operation, or all in one operation. The times are estimated for each operation and the estimator's assessment would include the most economical method.

The estimator will also consider scrap. Depending on the manufacturing processes employed, a certain number of pieces are unavoidably damaged. Typically, when tools are 'set up', faults such as chipped dies or mismatches are not discovered until some test pieces have been run and checked, and a quantity are made which are unusable. By experience, the estimator can establish what percentage of the total run this will be and the supplier should be given an allowance for this. This does not cover 'clippings' or 'frets' which are pieces of steel cut off in the pressing process. These are the supplier's responsibility. The estimator will also consider the 'setting-up time', which is the period where the press is out of production while being prepared to make the subject batch of items.

Normally the estimator assumes the minutes cost of each operation in labour minutes, as for example:

1. labour rate – £8 per hour (0.133 per minute);
2. overhead – 150% of labour minutes (0.20 per minute);
3. unit cost of steel;
4. scrap rate – 5%;
5. profit – 10%;
6. carriage – 10p each.

Thus, on the preceding factors the estimate may be as below.

1. Formula (i) $\dfrac{\text{Cost of tonne of steel}}{\text{Number of components produceable}}$ = £1.00 each

2. Formula (ii) Estimated percentage of scrap provided = 5% = £0.05 each

3. Operations
   (a) Blank 2 minutes @ £8 per hour
   (b) Pierce 1 minute @ £8 per hour
   (c) Form 2 minutes @ £8 per hour
   } * = £0.66 each

* The estimator would also consider 'methoding' in considering lowest ultimate cost (LUC) and recommend that only potential suppliers who would carry out the production phase in a single operation should be considered.

4. Formula (iii)

Overhead		
150% of	labour minutes	£1.00
	Works cost	£2.71
	Profit 10%	£0.27
	Total	£2.98
	Carriage	£0.10
(Profit is not taken on carriage)	Price delivered	= £3.08 each

Setting-up charge: 4 hours @ £15 per hour = £60

Clearly, if the supplier was going to produce the component in one operation, labour and overhead, and the size of profit are all reduced; thus the estimator provides a vital function in achieving lowest ultimate cost, by giving the buyer a target based, not on three operations, but one.

Without this support, the buyer might have gone to three suppliers who would have planned the job in the way the first estimate shows and selected a supplier slightly cheaper than the other two, when the *real price* – properly engineered – could be reduced to:

Cost of steel	£1.000
Scrap	£0.050
Blank, pierce, form – 3 minutes at £8 per hour (one operation)	£0.400
Overhead 150% of labour minutes	£0.600
WORKS COST	£2.050
PROFIT 10%	£0.205
TOTAL	£2.255
CARRIAGE	£0.100
PRICE DELIVERED	£2.355

Setting-up charge: 4 hours @ £15 per hour = £60

This is a most important aspect of supplier assessment and the efficiency of their capital equipment and processes is a vital part of selecting the right sources, often this cannot be uncovered without the use of an estimating targeting system.

In order to make this system work to its potential, the key items (those which contribute to the 80% of spend) should, at the time that the buyer is putting out enquiries, also be submitted for an estimate from the estimators.

Ideally, the buyer should then be able to compare the estimate with the quotations received and then open negotiations with suppliers to meet or beat the estimate, with the estimator's support if necessary.

PRODUCT COST CONTROL

Procedure number 2 (in Chapter 3) referred to the buyer's responsibility to inform designers when the price of a redesign is more expensive then the item it replaces.

The innumerable occasions when the writer has seen a new model being launched at a loss because the buyers have failed to take action to warn The Company lead to a belief that Product Cost Control should be part of the Purchasing function.

Frequently, the process for introducing new models starts from Sales and Marketing, comparing potential sales with actual sales and formulating a plan to either increase sales, or hold market share. The intention behind the plan is to increase profit by making the product more attractive to the potential customer.

One frequently used tactic is for Marketing to list a series of desirable improvements which would help sell the product. Often this takes the form of extra features which could be offered without change to the selling price or, alternatively, for only a small increase in price, giving the customer a range of benefits which have cost considerably less than the extra the customer is being asked to pay.

It may be decided that on the Road-Burner saloon car, the following features could allow market penetration to rise by 10% if they could be incorporated for less than £50:

1. improved braking;
2. improved upholstery and better back support for the seats;
3. a redesigned instrument panel;
4. an improved steering wheel;
5. more internal luggage storage;
6. new wheel trims.

The incorporation of these features would allow the price to rise by £300, then the company objective becomes 'to sell 10% more road-burners at £300 each more for an outlay of less than £50 per car'. The face-lifted road-burner Mk II should be launched in 12 months' time.

The objectives are thus clearly set and the design engineers get to work.

Now the current prices for the equipment which has been earmarked for change are:

1. Brakes, hydraulics and linkages	£250
2. Current upholstery and seats	£100
3. Current instrument panel and instruments	£150
4. Current steering wheel	£10
5. Current internal luggage storage, in-door panels and instrument panel and boot	£40
6. Wheel trims	£20
TOTAL	£570

If the changes allowable are maximum £50, then each of the six features can only rise from current prices by 8.8% – or at least the bottom line must not increase by more than 8.8%.

The design engineers on brakes have always wanted to improve the braking, the group on internal trim welcome the chance to improve and so do the other engineering groups, so that once off the leash, with little idea of actual costs and the condition of the buying market, produce schemes which Marketing and Sales enthuse over and ask for yet more improvements which the designers willingly incorporate.

Unless their designs have been submitted to estimators and buyers who agree that these enhancements can be obtained for less than £50, the designs will be released for purchase and disaster is less than 12 months away!

Product Cost Control should see each of these additions while they are still on the drawing board and prepare preliminary estimates, thus:

	Current price £	Estimated additional cost of change £
1. Brakes, hydraulics and linkages	250	90
2. Current upholstery and seats	100	20
3. Current instrument panel and instruments	150	27
4. Current steering wheel	10	2
5. Current internal luggage storage and boot	40	6
6. Wheel trims	20	5
	£570	£150

This is three times the target!

BACK TO THE DRAWING BOARD

The designers now know that they have designed too richly so they seek to eliminate some parts of their original design in order to come down to the cost target.

Time is now becoming a problem because Purchasing have indicated their lead times as requiring release by anything up to six months prior to the planned launch date.

As the releases for the various groups start to arrive in Purchasing, their target is to try to buy the new features for 8.8% more as a maximum than their current price. (Many detailed negotiations take place at this stage between purchasing and their suppliers.)

The brakes and hydraulics buyer finds that the suppliers' price cannot be reduced below 10% cost increase and agrees that the extra features in the brakes *do* merit a 10% increase; the buyer then refers back to product cost control with the question, 'Do I place this order – because lead time is so short that if I don't place right now, the Road-Burner Mk II will go on the road without any brakes at all!'

The designers say that they have reduced the modifications as far as they possibly can, so the order has to be placed.

Of the £50 allowable, half has gone on the brakes alone.

Fortunately, the upholstery comes in at a dead 8.8% increase and the instrument panel changes come in at a 5% increase only. This means that there is only £8.70 in the kitty to cover changes to the steering wheel, internal luggage storage and wheel trims, which have not yet been released.

THE TARGET CAN BE ACHIEVED

Product Cost Control must now meet with Engineering and Marketing to decide if the changes still on the drawing board can be achieved within the £8.70 which is left.

(In fact, as the original estimates for these last three only showed a potential £13 per model cost, the problem is not too desperate.) Product cost, by exerting pressure on the designers, the buyers and marketing, can influence the amount of design work and the activity of the buyers to hit the target and have ensured successful achievement of the target.

In the writer's opinion, the best place to position Product Cost Control is within purchasing and, as will be seen in this example, without product cost control, the original designs would have probably achieved the penetration target, but would have failed to hit the profit target.

The writer has seen many cases where, because model costs were not controlled and the linkages between Design, Marketing and Purchasing were not maintained, huge losses were sustained by manufacturers.

It is Purchasing's responsibility to tell any requisitioner that they are asking for a too expensive product and Product Cost Control in Purchasing is the mechanism to do it.

10

NEGOTIATION METHODS

The Duke of Wellington once asked a young cavalry subaltern, 'What is the main purpose of the cavalry in war?'

To which the young sprig of the nobility replied, 'To add tone, Sir, to what would otherwise be a vulgar brawl!'

Of course he should have replied, 'To be the eyes and ears of the Army'.

The role of the cavalry in reconnaissance has passed in these days to the Air Forces, and to Radar – but the pressing demand always for the successful Commander in the field is to establish the enemy's intentions before committing himself in order to achieve his objectives.

The buying negotiator has the same problem – how to establish the intentions of the opponent and, in the face of these, to achieve the buyer's own objectives.

Thus just as the General has an objective to capture strategic positions and limit the enemy's ability to make war, the buyer's objective is to obtain the company requirements at the lowest ultimate cost and in the deployment of the buyer's purchasing power, to obtain the benefits sought.

In Chapter 8, 'Supplier – Friend or Foe?, the discussion centred around the supplier's strategy and the supplier's tactics.

Many of the sections of the other chapters have been an introduction to the weapons available to you to achieve the lowest ultimate cost objective. In this chapter, the conflicting objectives meet and the buyer's weapons are shown in action.

NEGOTIATION PLANNING

To go into a negotiation, you should have:

1. an estimate for some at least of the key items;
2. a savings/losses plan;
3. an economic forecast;
4. a recent supplier's balance sheet/company annual report;
5. competitive quotations;
6. a supplier performance report;
7. inventory report.

But you still may not know what the lowest ultimate cost could be.

CASE 1

In the forecast which was prepared in Chapter 4, one of the suppliers who it was forecast would be pressing you for a price increase would be a particularly difficult nut to crack.

The supplier was Able Limited, a press worker with whom you spend £600 000 per annum, and they are claiming a 4% price increase. The cost to you over a full year would be £24 000 and they have asked for the price increase to be effective as at the seventh month (exactly as forecast) – but you had forecast the full year effect as 3.3%, i.e. £19 800 – so why is the supplier asking for 4%? – you could, of course, reject it out of hand as being unreasonable – but knowing Able Limited, you decide you will meet them with a set-piece negotiation.

Another reason could be that their propaganda (sales policy?) states that they look on £600 000 per annum spend as a small account and they get rougher treatment than their bigger customers. This could have been said to encourage the company to place more business with them – but it could be the truth!

ASSEMBLING THE INFORMATION

The bringing together of this information, together with your knowledge of their quality and supply performance (which statistics show is far from perfect), demonstrates some of the lines you will eventually use in the negotiation. It also will demonstrate that some more work must be done before you sit down to negotiate.

Table 10.1 Able Limited – Key items

Part number	Current price £	Best competition £	Competition tool cost £	Annual volume	Estimate £	Current annual cost £	Best competition £	
1. MW1234	5.50	5.30	10 000	17 454	5.20	96 000	92 506	Baker Limited
2. MW2468	15.00	14.20	20 000	9 600	14.00	144 000	136 320	Baker Limited
3. MW2500	22.00	22.10	17 000	2 182	22.50	48 000	48 222	Jig Limited
4. MW3900	3.00	2.40	3 000	22 000	2.20	66 000	52 800	Sugar Limited
5. MW2036	9.00	6.80	10 000	14 000	7.00	126 000	95 200	Tare Limited
			60 000			480 000	425 048	(11.2%)
20 Minor Pressings						120 000		

DEVELOPMENT OF TACTICS

1. First, the comparison of best competitive prices is a selection from quotations for the whole of Able's business from their four competitors, all of whom are already suppliers to you. Note that item 4 appears *under-priced* as both the estimate and the best quote are above Able's price.

   Selecting best quotes in this way is often known as 'cherry-picking', and since the suppliers themselves tend to look at bottom lines in their quotes, they may well assume that like Able's item 4, it doesn't matter if some individual items are 'keen', provided the bottom line is satisfactory.

   They may not continue to offer these prices if they do not get all the business! You should endeavour, even if you decide to negotiate at 'bottom line', to ensure that all items have a 'stand-alone' price.
2. The tool costs total £60 000 and although unit prices from the best quotes would save 11.2%, unless you could amortize tooling

over, say, three years, your savings would be virtually wiped out if you had to pay the whole tool costs in the current year.

e.g.	Current price	£480 000 + 4% request	= £499 200
	Best price	£425 048 + £60 000 tooling	= £485 048

If you were able to eliminate the 4% price increase, it would still be worth while to re-tool, if you could amortize the tooling.

3. Therefore, you need to talk to Baker, Jig, Sugar and Tare to suggest that they should consider amortizing their tooling over three years.
4. You can assume that whatever result you arrive at on your key items will follow through on to your non-key items, so items 1 to 5 are your field of negotiation and as they represent 80% of turnover, the detail of the non-key items can form a subsequent negotiation with the chosen source. If, for example, you achieved 11.2% reduction on the key items, you would demand the same reduction on the non-key items.
5. In your forecast, your aim was to avoid a PPV bulge as discussed in Chapter 4, and this is an important objective.
6. First quotes from competition

	Unit Cost	Tool Cost	Total Year One Only
Baker Limited	£450 000	£70 000	£520 000
Sugar Limited	£465 000	£75 000	£540 000
Tare Limited	£455 000	£60 000	£515 000
Jig Limited	£449 000	£55 000	£504 000

(After second discussions with competitive sources.)

7. Second quotes from competition with three-year amortization

	Unit Cost	Amortized × 3 Years Tool Cost	
Baker Limited	£450 000	£23 333	£473 333 p.a.
Sugar Limited	£465 000	£25 000	£490 000 p.a.
Tare Limited	£455 000	£20 000	£475 000 p.a.
Jig Limited	£449 000	£18 333	£467 333 p.a.

8. Jig obviously offers the best bottom line, comparing this with £480 000 (current Able price). But if Able could be made to meet

the best quotes, an 11.2% reduction to £425 048 is possible, whereas resourcing to Jig Limited would only yield 8.8%.

9. If you were put into a position where it appeared you must resource the whole of Able's work (which would fit in with your plans to reduce the number of suppliers and increase clout with some, or all, of the remainder), a major concern would be how fast could Jig re-tool 25 pressings, obtain sample approval and get into production? Also, could their tool room cope with all these tools quickly?

   It would appear that since Able would need their tools to produce until Jig took over, tool transfer is not an option, so at least three months would have to elapse before Jig could 'go' on all 25 items. Therefore, you would have to persuade Able Limited to maintain their old prices for three months. Alternatively, try to tool up with Jig without telling Able, the danger being that Able might find out too soon.

CHOICE OF OBJECTIVES

1. Able Limited to withdraw price increase.
2. Able Limited to reduce prices by 11.2%.
3. If Able does not accept 1 and 2 (or a near match, i.e. a 10% reduction would be acceptable), negotiate a three-month stay of price increases while Jig is tooled up.
4. Reinvestigate cherry-picking and source Able's materials among all four other sources.

SUPPLIER'S OBJECTIVES

1. The accountants have told sales they need a price increase if they are to justify a new share issue.
2. Able therefore must fight hard to obtain increases from their customers.
3. Policy is to press the smaller customers hardest.
4. They need, however, to hold on to as much of their business that they can, since they may otherwise not be attractive on the market if it gets around that they're losing business.
5. They believe that the new purchasing manager may be a soft touch and is keen to make an impression on his or her own management. The manager may be therefore scared of making too many waves since Able Limited have consistently courted

quite a number of amateur buyers in The Company who could be used to cry 'stinking fish' about the new purchasing manager's decision if it went against Able!

POWER AND COERCION

Your secretary has just told you that Mr P. Plant, sales director of Able Limited, is waiting to see you, so three final tips.

1. Keep control of the meeting. Don't let Mr Plant register his request for a price increase until you have registered your discontent with his:
   - supply performance;
   - quality performance.
2. Next, tell him that you have been carrying out studies in the market and he is 11.2% uncompetitive on price.
3. You are offering them a last chance by bidding competitively to keep the work they've got and, if the new quote is uncompetitive, then you will be forced to resource.
4. Then you can ask, 'What did you come to see me for Mr Plant?'

The planning which you have done has made you pretty fire-proof. He may decide not to present his request for a 4% increase or may offer to withdraw it immediately if there has been previous correspondence on the subject – then you must insist on a re-quote to be received by you as soon as possible.

This is power and coercion negotiation and, provided your research is thorough, as the example under discussion, your reconnaissance and planning will invariably allow you to play the power and coercion game.

PARTNERSHIP NEGOTIATION?

This was not the only way to play this particular situation. You could have simply stated that your estimators feel there was more than a 10% reduction possible – as indeed there is – since the lowest ultimate cost is a perpetually moving target – and that prior to considering resourcing, you would like your estimators to investigate his manufacturing methods. The benefits to Able Limited would be that if they accepted your recommendations, your prices would reduce but he would apply the new methods to his other customers and improve his profit margin with them.

This might make it easier to allow Able to save face – but in a case like this, the direct challenge has the value of being a shock tactic and you may feel Able should not be given too much room for face-saving.

IS THE SUPPLIER WILLING TO NEGOTIATE?

Both of these methods depend on his wanting to keep the business, but he might tell you to 'go and visit the nearest taxidermist!'

In which case, you must consider if he might stop production immediately – possibly your terms and conditions should have a termination agreement (say three months either side), but if you refer to Clause 11, Clause 16 and Clause 19 in the draft terms and conditions in Chapter 3, all of those show that you are within your rights to take the action of refusing his price request and requesting reductions, and continuing to discuss new prices.

Your actions would not give him the legal right to stop production just like that.

Despite telling you what you can do to yourself, he must discuss this matter with his board and come back to you with the company's reaction.

After he has given you his final answer, you should ethically tell Mr Plant what you are going to do, and remember, if he has any schedule liabilities in raw materials or stock, you must take these.

Then you must resource.

But, more likely, he will want to negotiate and you will know exactly what you want to obtain from him. The most probable outcome would be that he would withdraw his price increase request and offer some concessions – but you must stick to your guns – you are not in the business of financing other companies' aims.

Dealing with the unexpected

Sadly, for the buyer, there are occasions when your forecasting lets you down. Competitive enquiries are inconclusive, your estimators can't give you a clear guide, and a totally unexpected problem gets up and hits you between the eyes.

The unexpected can be one of any of the following events:

1. massive price increase in a raw material;
2. sudden bankruptcy of a previously solid supply source;
3. fire at a supplier's or at your own works;

4. strike at supplier's or at your own works;
5. supplier stopping supplies due to The Company being behind with payment;
6. design engineers wanting urgently to set up a contract with a supplier that they claim is the only one and the supplier wants a contract before starting the design and development they want;
7. massive quality rejections of material urgently required for production.

There will be others not listed above which will stand up and bite you during your professional life, and you will learn that some need not have been unexpected and, from experience, you will learn how to deal with them. There are other events that shouldn't have happened to a dog, but you've had it happen to you!

Time is the biggest factor to be considered. Questioning, which is a major part of negotiation, and listening to the answers, is often the rescuer of the buyer.

THE FOUR QUESTIONS

Each of the seven examples can be quantified by the answers to four questions.

1. When does this event affect sales/production?
2. How does it affect sales/production?
3. What are my options to avoid sales/production being jeopardized?
4. Can I deploy my options inside the time limit the answer to question 1 gives me?

CASE 2

Massive increase in price of a raw material

Questions 1 and 2 are easily quantifiable. Price increases affect the customer immediately inventory at the old price becomes exhausted and the price increase alone will not affect production but it *will* affect profit, so you *must* act.

Attitude change involving emotion

If you have no competition which is viable, then you must try another technique with the supplier. This seeks to change the supplier's attitude by the use of emotion, however, if the supplier is a 'hard case', anguished appeals such as those prefaced with phases like, 'Surely you can . . .' and, 'We'll all be in trouble if you don't', or 'My boss will . . .', will cut no ice – but if you try it, be convincing!

If you don't feel you can get away with it, you can try the following.

Search for a middle ground compromise

Perhaps you can suggest to the supplier that your customers will need time to adjust to the new prices and if you put up your price too quickly, then not only would the company lose business but the raw material supplier would also. Probably the supplier could apply the increases in stages over say one year. This would help mitigate the price increase (and incidentally give you time to look for a second source or ask design engineering to help find a substitute and less expensive material), and ensure that you and the raw material supplier can still earn some money.

The other technique that is available to you is the following.

Trading mutually advantageous concessions

What does the supplier want which would satisfy the requirement for a price increase?

1. Extra turnover by offering other raw materials?
2. Bigger batch deliveries, reducing delivery costs?
3. Payment at 14 days instead of 60 days etc.?

Each one of the items you could offer could be priced and must again result in mitigating the size of the increase.

So the four negotiation techniques are:

1. power and coercion;
2. attitude change involving emotion;
3. search for middle ground compromise;
4. trading mutually advantageous concessions.

Every negotiation technique known is a variant of one of the above.

CASE 3

A supplier who is vital to you has gone bankrupt.

Unless your ongoing research into the financial health of all of your suppliers is very reliable, the day will arrive when one of your buyers will burst into your office saying, 'Jig Limited has just been declared bankrupt!'

Again, you ask the four questions, paying particular attention to number 3 – What are your options?

- It would be possible to re-tool all their work elsewhere, but time would have run out long before the tooling was ready.
- The tooling may be your property but the Receiver will demand proof that you have ownership of the tools before you can take them away. Besides which, the Official Receiver wants to keep the business going while finding a buyer – and if you take your tooling away, it reduces the saleability of the supplier – so the Receiver will be resistant.
- Is the Official Receiver prepared to run the tools to produce your requirements until another buyer can be found?

Invariably in order to maintain your supplies, you will find yourself negotiating with the official receiver, 'trading mutually advantageous concessions'. The receiver may ask for you to buy the raw material and reduce the selling prices of the supplier's materials to you accordingly, and you may be asked for payment in 30 days instead of 60 etc.

Most times, you will be able to reach a satisfactory compromise by trading concessions and your material supply will be secure again.

CASE 4

Fire at a supplier's works or your own.

If one of your suppliers has a fire they are probably going to be unable to supply you for several days; if they tell you they won't be able to restart for a week and all their customers need supplies within 10 days, your objective must be to ensure that your requirements are met before your run-out dates.

You may be able to use power and coercion – 'If you don't meet my dates, I shall resource all my work away from you' – or you could trade for mutually advantageous concessions.

What does your supplier need most at the moment?

Could it be the loan of machine tools, new raw material or labour? Each of these could persuade your supplier to make sure that whatever happens your needs will be catered for, even to the exclusion of other customers.

If the fire is at your works, your needs could be the same as those of your supplier and you will have to use all four techniques from obtaining loans of machine tools to obtaining unscheduled requirements in double-quick time.

CASE 5

Strike at supplier's, or your own, works.

First, you must not, under any circumstances, apply pressure to the supplier in order to get them to cave into demands from the strikers.

From a point of view of self-interest as a buyer, you could be supporting the supplier's later claims for price increases, and secondly, what if their workers succeed in getting a pay rise thanks to your help and your own workers get to hear of what you've done?

You don't, however, sit on your hands. You are entitled (see '*Force majeure*' in the Glossary) to take whatever steps you consider needful in order to keep your workers supplied.

It is possible, by talking to your suppliers, to assess well beforehand whether they might be having a strike at wage bargaining time. If there is a suspicion, then the supplier may well be able to say, 'It won't last longer than a fortnight', then you increase your inventory to stand-off the period foreseen. You then reduce back to normal after the supplier's labour return to work. So you need to check regularly with the supplier on the industrial relations climate.

On the other hand, if your works are on strike, your suppliers have built, in all good faith, your next month's supply and you cannot accept it because the factory is closed, you are back to the four negotiation techniques in order to keep material out and avoid any sort of price increase which may occur either then or at a later date as a result of their loss of earnings during your strike.

CASE 6

A supplier puts you on 'stop' and refuses to deliver until invoices currently with the company are paid in full.

If you can persuade accounts to part with the money it's the end of the problem, but what if they can only pay part of the outstanding invoices?

You can use the fact that you can immediately offer some of the debt the supplier is owed in order to reach a middle ground compromise – also attitude change by emotion can work to get them to re-start supplies.

But if The Company are going to continue to play this despicable game, then you must look for another supplier; since most suppliers will not accept being played about with for long!

CASE 7

The designers have just been told by a 'black-box' supplier that it will take 16 months to design and develop a new black-box that has to cut into production in 18 months' time, and the supplier has said that they will not start work until they have 'a piece of paper' in their hand authorizing them to do it, and to be paid for it.

Ask the four questions and then review your methods of negotiation. (The type of contract will be discussed in a later chapter.)

What are your techniques going to be?

1. Power and coercion? The supplier is using it on you!
2. Attitude change involving emotion? By the sound of it, the supplier is using the design engineers to generate the emotion!
3. Search for middle ground compromise? 'If I give you, Mr Supplier, the contract, I want control over price by material, labour and overhead content, and development time; I will pay at a certain rate but I want to see all invoices and weekly time sheets before I authorize payment – at 60 days?'

   Remember the supplier, too, wants the contract for development – knowing probably that you have no competition at this stage – but that doesn't mean that you will not instruct your engineers to develop a new source as soon as the supplier has left the design office.
4. Trading mutually advantageous concessions? The supplier wants the contract – you want control of cost. Some of your controls could be of benefit to them so you may be able to get them to suggest other benefits they can offer. Listen carefully.

CASE 8

Massive rejections by Quality Control of supplier's material.

In Chapter 1, the techniques used by the inspection team were established so you will know if there is a chance that there is, in among the material that has been rejected, the possibility of using some while other arrangements are being explored. This may require piece-by-piece inspection.

You may have to use one of the four techniques on the quality manager in order to get agreement on this!

With regard to the supplier, you have only two techniques available.

1. Power and coercion. 'You have dropped us in it by supplying reject material – I want OK material here by the end of today!'
2. Attitude change involving emotion. The supplier may say, 'I don't believe the situation is as bad as you say, and I want to have them all back before I do anything else.'

   A really good angry outburst will often shift recalcitrant suppliers and here is a very good opening to deploy it.

In this chapter you have seen in Case 1 the set-piece battle and, in the other seven cases, serious skirmishes which are all very common occurrences.

Each of the eight skirmishes can be foreseen and planned for, and the heat taken out of them, by establishing plans and methods to deal with these situations before they arise – the only exceptions are the real acts of God.

PRECAUTIONS

Don't allow yourself to struggle through the situations that have been discussed in this chapter without setting up precautions for the future and reviewing your actions to see what improvements are possible, as follows.

1. Unexpected raw material increases – good forecasting and research techniques would have told you this was likely to happen several months before and you would have already been searching for alternative suppliers and alternative materials.
2. The same applies to the sudden bankruptcy of a vital supplier. This situation becomes obvious long before it actually happens. Research pays!
3. Fires and acts of God – the real surprises! – but strikes are not, and *can* be forecast and appropriate action taken beforehand.
4. Going on 'stop' with a supplier – the purchasing manager should know perpetually how supplier payment is proceeding and be forearmed, or seeing that the situation is corrected.
5. Design engineers should never be allowed to be dealing with

suppliers without Purchasing input and involvement for the new product requirements. No single source should be given a development contract which requires payment for work done. What should happen is that two sources are given the opportunity to develop the product – the winner gets the production quantities, the loser gets nothing.

If both are accepted, then dual sourcing is a possibility and both suppliers have gained business by their 'up-front' *free* development.

6. Massive rejections. What do we have a Quality Assurance programme for? Clearly it's not working somehow – it must be rectified for the future.

LISTENING PAYS

In all this framework of near conflict, the most important tools negotiators have are their ears.

Very recently, the writer did a considerable amount of research for a very rare raw material used in certain defence equipment and was only able to uncover one source worldwide, which was based in the USA.

Enquiries were launched and a quote received.

Since the raw material was so rare and there was no apparent competition, the writer had no idea if the price was fair or not. Since this was required for a product with a tight selling price and this material played an important part in the cost build-up, the writer decided to try to reduce the price of the material.

The supplier duly arrived in the writer's office and after a few minutes, the writer decided he'd better get on with it, and said, 'Presumably you sell a lot of this material?'

'Yes', said the supplier, 'but this is a very interesting contract and we are most anxious to get it.'

NOTE: 'Most anxious to get the contract'!

'Well', said the writer, 'looking at this price, I would have felt that it wasn't of that much interest to you.'

Silence.

'Have you had a quote from our competitor, the ABC Company of Detroit?' asked the supplier.

NOTE: There *is* a second source – the ABC Company of Detroit!

The writer, 'Well, I shall be talking to them later today.'

NOTE: The Absolute Truth!

Silence.

The supplier, 'So you *are* in contact with them, I wondered if you might be – look, I'll take 20% off my price if I can be sure of getting the contract.'

NOTE: This made our selling price of the product *much* more profitable.

The writer, 'This certainly puts you in the frame and I will undertake to let you know by the end of the week if you've got the contract – I'm still not too happy about the price.'

NOTE: Try again!

The supplier, 'Well, that's my very best shot and I hope your answer will be in the affirmative.'

NOTE: That appears to be the supplier's bottom price!

The writer was left wondering whether he had been the subject of a really good (and new) sales pitch or whether the American supplier wasn't accustomed to being listened to.

Three telephone calls to Detroit revealed that the ABC Company could not get anywhere near the first supplier's price or delivery.

Needless to say, the contract was then placed with alacrity, but I have to confess I don't know if I did hit the lowest ultimate cost!!

Clearly, the reader will be able to see the mistakes the sales representative made – most effective was the two periods of silence where the supplier rushed in and said more than he should have done.

Buyers make this mistake all the time by 'rushing in', but the art of good listening is as vital to the art of good buying as good pre-negotiation planning.

11

COST REDUCTION TECHNIQUES, MARKET RESEARCH, IMPORTATION AND INCOTERMS

In Chapter 10, the discussion was about the implementation of strategy by the deployment of suitable tactics using pure negotiation methods.

The same purchasing manager, who used to refer to suppliers as 'Fair weather friends', talked also in boxing metaphors, and he would have called Chapter 10 a dissertation on 'fancy footwork' and the matter in this chapter as the 'slogging match'.

Fancy footwork (to use his expression) is a highly effective and conclusive method, but what if, in the negotiation with Able Limited, your decision was to put your estimators into Able's press shop and fabrications shop to examine their production methods, times, metal handling and inspection techniques? After two months' study, they found that if production methods were updated, times could be reduced, metal handling would be improved and inspection techniques overhauled, and that these actions would save you only 9%.

Let us say that the supplier agreed to accept your recommendations – what would you then do?

It would probably not be worth the candle to resource and the knowledge you have now obtained on material, labour, overhead and profit will be invaluable to control Able Limited in the future but, despite all these good things, you're still looking for 11.2% instead of 9%.

A saving of 2.2% at least still eludes you and if you can save another £15 000, then it's worth another shot.

There are two processes which can be deployed. Both require input from the design engineers of The Company, the estimators/production engineers of The Company and the production engineers of the supplier.

VALUE ANALYSIS

The first technique is value analysis. The process is to select a component and analyse it from the viewpoint of design and function.

An often quoted example is the ordinary common or garden teaspoon. Until the 1950s, a tea shop or restaurant served tea with brass teaspoons coated with electroplated nickel silver (EPNS), and the most exclusive served tea with silver spoons. Of course, such spoons used to get stolen and replacement costs were significant.

The next generation of teaspoons (about 1965) were made of pressed stainless steel – less expensive than EPNS but they served the same purpose, and these too got stolen by the thousand. Then, in the 1970s, granulated sugar was replaced in restaurants by either shakers or cubes wrapped in paper. The last teaspoons were thin plastic models of their metal forerunners. The function of the teaspoon was reduced – from being a small sugar shovel and stirrer – to just a stirrer. Now, a sliver of plastic suffices to stir tea or coffee and, provided it doesn't melt in a very hot drink, it serves its purpose well.

It is an education to look at any component and ask the team to consider ways of more closely matching function to design. If, moving across the tea table, one examines a cup and saucer we see that the saucer is becoming redundant, and how long will it be before the handle disappears from the cup and the decoration disappears? Yet, what remains is a plain cup with no handle and no decoration, which is perfectly fit for the function of drinking.

Thus, value analysis consists of comparing function to value on an existing component.

Comparing a post-war tea shop where a cup, saucer and teaspoon valued at today's prices as, say, £4, has its function replaced by a plastic cup and 'stirrer' valued at, say £1 per thousand. Value analysis has proved its point.

A programme to examine each of Able's components supplied to the company would undoubtedly show significant results.

Value analysis can also be used in the manufacturing process by the elimination of unnecessary operations in the production methods. A typical example is the machining of bar-turned items where the workpiece is machined overall, when in fact only the ends need to be machined.

VALUE ENGINEERING

Value engineering is applied when a component is being designed. The forum can be the same, namely The Company's designers, production engineers and purchasing, together with the potential supplier's production engineers.

Here, the objective is to avoid unnecessary cost being engendered by the designer taking sufficient cognizance of the methods which will have to be used in manufacturing.

In the days when the draughtsperson served an apprenticeship on the shop floor, before ever being allowed near a drawing board, this process (value engineering) was not so necessary as it is now.

If one takes a sample 100 drawings emanating from a design office these days, possibly up to 10 will be unable to be made at all because metal cannot behave in the way the designer has drawn it. For example, if metal is drawn too tight around a bend it will split at the bend. You will see drawings which ignore this basic principle.

Another 10 drawings will have a working part which has to be machined to a very tight tolerance in one small area. The rest is out in air and perhaps only needs cleaning off. Unless someone jogs the designer's metaphorical elbow, those drawings will demand that the whole component should be machined overall to the same tight tolerance or finish.

A large number of drawings will omit the material from which the component is to be made. Where components which are required to be cast are involved, the designer forgets that patterns have to be opened after casting and will design in such a way that mould lines will appear right where they are not wanted.

Value engineering is a vital tool in the business of cost avoidance and very often it is the purchasing manager who has to be the initiator of the system.

Of course, value engineering is not going to help you with getting that extra 2% from Able Limited, at least not now – but if value analysis hasn't found it for you, there is another technique which can be applied.

VALUE ADMINISTRATION

This process goes by several different names, often including the word 'rationalization'.

The forum can be the same as in the previous two techniques, but value administration looks at the shop floor with the aim of making the labour force more productive.

Take, for example, the inspector who is stationed at the end of a production line and whose role it is to inspect the product coming off that line.

If the line is running well, there are no rejects and the inspector is, for long periods of the day, being unproductive. The operators within the cycle times of their machines also have periods of down-time. By fairly simple methods, the operators can be trained to inspect their own work during the 'down-time' and the inspector redeployed.

On a machine shop production line, do you really need charge-hands, foremen and a superintendent? You may well extend your study to this level in your quest for reduced prices out of Able Limited.

Often, by a combination of value analysis and value adminis-tration, it is possible to redesign tooling so that the operator is making components in multiples, i.e. four at a time instead of one at a time, which reduces the labour element, increases productivity and the only on-cost which is quickly offset, is in modified tooling.

Of course these are the 'slogging' battles against unnecessary cost, and they take time and effort, they also tie up valuable resources, but they reduce cost on visible examples and lower base prices for the future.

Their most important function is that they spearhead the search for the lowest ultimate cost and this is where purchasing should always be the driving force.

OVERSEAS PURCHASING

French industrial buyers suffer from a disease which they joke about, but recognize as a real problem and they call it the 'Quadrilateral Syndrome'. France is geographically a quadrilateral and they are loath to buy outside it. They're not that keen to buy even from Belgium! This is often interpreted as parochialism, but in fact they are no different from the British buyer who announced proudly to the writer recently, 'All my suppliers are within 40 miles of my factory and if any of them are in trouble, I can be there inside an hour.'

Italian buyers don't like to buy outside their own region and get very nervous if it is suggested that they should buy from France or the UK.

The average American or Canadian buyer really never considers Europe as a supply source, in fact Canadian buyers don't even like buying from the US because of the exchange rate differences between the US and the Canadian dollar, and the US buyer tends to look on the Canadians as provincial and a little backward.

Apart from the fear that they all have that they dare not be too far geographically from their suppliers in case of panics, they are also handicapped by language limitations and their lack of interest in having to get involved in different exchange rates, customs and taxes which they see as profitless hassle.

Yet each of these nations has proud histories as explorers and traders with far-off customers and should not have to suffer from parochial buyers. Each of these nations also sets out to export to each other and the rest of the world.

The fundamental need of a company that is going to export to the rest of the world is that their prices should be worldwide competitive. A company with 'parochial' buyers does not give itself a real chance unless its buyers can satisfy themselves that their components and materials are being bought at worldwide competitive prices.

Market research

So how does the buyer who really wants to make sure that his or her company's purchases really are worldwide competitive go about it?

From the range of components and raw material purchases that were established in Chapter 1, we know that the major part of the buy is in:

Castings	£2 000 000 per annum
Pressings	£3 000 000 per annum
Electrics and electronics	£7 000 000 per annum
Rubber mouldings	£1 000 000 per annum
Forgings	£1 000 000 per annum
Standard parts	£2 000 000 per annum

Paint	£1 000 000 per annum
Copper	£1 000 000 per annum
Steel	£2 000 000 per annum

If you then look at these items in terms of technology, the highest technological purchases are in the electrical/electronic group. Castings, forgings and pressings are lower-tech items. Rubber mouldings are probably lower tech still and, apart from paint, the rest are raw materials.

These are various descriptions for the different levels of technological development in the world, some speak of First, Second and Third Worlds, while others speak of Developed Countries and Least Developed Countries (LDCs).

Some of your component areas are labour intensive, others based on a ready supply of raw materials, others still are the by-product of highly mechanized processes.

It is possible by requesting meetings with the commercial attachés of the relevant embassies and consulates to obtain much good, solid information on such matters as labour rates, access to raw materials, governmental support schemes, both in export benefits and countertrade opportunities, and their production specialities.

This research is more appropriate with the least developed countries than North America, Western Europe and Japan, but is of surprisingly good value in researching into these countries too, although much other information is readily available.

From this research, it will emerge that certain countries are in fact specializing in limited areas of production development. Some European and North American companies are already established in Korea, Malaya, Singapore, India, Hong Kong, China, Indonesia, Taiwan, South America, West Indies etc., some by having buying departments established there and others by establishing manufacturing facilities there. Also, these countries have a rapidly developing indigenous industry.

Another point of interest is that many countries now will argue that if they are to buy British exports, then they would like, or prefer that, part of the content of the British product should have some native material within it. The reason is simple in their eyes, 'Why should they spend their hard-earned currency on imports to the exclusion of local industry?'

From your research, you can see that some countries offer the possibility of finding good products at very attractive prices. There are many countries in the world where high quality labour earns perhaps no more than £4 per week for a 40-hour week and, as you carry out your research, you will be astounded to find out how many there are.

From your research, you will have established lists of potential suppliers and you should launch enquiries which pick up on the specialities you have identified so that, for example, you would not look, say, for high-tech electronics in India when Japan is available – and so on.

With your enquiries, you should request plant lists, accessibility to sea ports and airports, and their willingness to export. The quotations of some of them you receive may seem unattractive and it is is here that you'd better start deciding what countries require a visit.

In all cases, face-to-face negotiations and discussions are very important, but when tackling the LDCs it is vital. In preparing for your visits, apart from obtaining visas where appropriate, and inoculations and vaccinations, make sure that you have a good brief on the behaviour that is an absolute 'no-no' in the countries you propose to visit and what they find acceptable.

For example, should you wear a conservative business suit, normally with a white shirt and black shoes in cooler weather or is a shirt and slacks, normally with a tie, acceptable in hot weather?

In Muslim nations, the rules of the Koran apply – smoking and drinking in public are not permitted. In Saudi Arabia, never show the sole of your shoes to anyone by, for example, sitting cross-legged – this is offensive.

In India, never offer anything to an Indian with your left hand – always use your right. Many Indians are strict vegetarians so be careful if, in a restaurant dining with Indians, that you check they will not be offended if you order a meat dish.

In China, coughing, spitting and belching in public are not at all offensive to the inhabitants, so it is unwise for a visitor to show that they find these habits offensive.

Despite all these provisos, everyone is interested in increasing their business with the West and they do try, in most cases, to recognize that you are from a different culture and try to accommodate you.

In Western Europe, a businesslike approach is expected, which differs very little to what you are accustomed to in the UK. In the writer's experience, French attitudes are the most close to those of the British, which is probably why there is sometimes a certain friction between the two nations. The French, in a negotiation, always want to have the bun but keep the penny, and so do the British!

The Italians are hard bargainers, and very skilful in a negotiation in making the tiniest concessions with the air of facing bankruptcy because of your unfeeling attitude. But don't let it fool you. Keep pushing (once you get used to negotiating with them it becomes good fun) and eventually you will get a good price.

Language skills are important even if you are not in the country of the origin of the language. For example, French (apart from in France) is spoken in large areas of Canada, Belgium, Africa and India. It is also the second language in parts of Italy and Spain.

German is useful in Eastern Europe; Italian is also spoken in other areas than Italy.

In all the LDCs, English is well known, although these days the American brand is more common than English English.

Once you have made contact with the potential suppliers, you must first of all satisfy yourself that their manufacturing methods and quality techniques are acceptable, but beware of rejecting good opportunities because their methods are different.

Your second concern is shipping.

British Embassies, or High Commissions, can give you excellent advice on shipping, duties etc. and you should be able to decide whether you want to place orders during your visit.

It may well be that on your visit, you may be approached by Government officials of the country you are in to discuss counter-trade.

COUNTER-TRADE

Imagine that you are perhaps in Poland and you have decided that although you would buy from a foundry, you cannot get the price you want. Normally, transport costs, insurance duties etc. dictate that you should not consider prices ex-works if there is less than a 35% difference between the local price and the price you are paying in the UK.

Poland, like most of the LDCs we have mentioned, is interested in obtaining hard currencies. If you were to buy from a Polish foundry you would be asked to pay in a hard currency and, as a UK buyer, you would be expected to pay in sterling. On the other hand, The Company sales staff would not accept zlotys but demand payment in a hard currency, US dollars, French francs, Deutschmarks, lira, pounds sterling, in fact, anything but zlotys.

Thus, the best hope Poland has to be able to buy hard currency goods is to earn sterling from their own exports.

With this in mind, your Polish foundry management will have

tried very hard to meet your price, but they may feel that they have products that you could sell for them in the UK and remit the sterling to them to allow them to buy imports from hard currency areas.

They will naturally pay a commission for this service. Obviously the commission they pay can contribute to the profit of The Company.

Apart from the opportunity to be able to buy at truly world competitive prices and improve your company's export potential, the use of counter-trade can be converted into creating more sales for The Company.

THE 'COLD-CALLING' REP

One of the toughest roles played in the Purchasing business is played by the sales representatives of those companies who spend their lives contacting potential new customers by calling on Purchasing departments.

There is nothing that tells you more about the quality of a Purchasing department than the entrance to the offices.

1. Some companies display notices such as:
   'No representatives will be seen without an appointment.'
   'Representatives are seen on Monday afternoons only.'
2. Others have glass cases with components displayed and a notice which says, 'Can you make this product cheaper than our current source? If so, speak to Mr Bloggs on extension 506.'

Both examples are admissions of failure.

If a representative calls, then someone in purchasing should see him or her. In five minutes, the representative can tell you what is being offered. If the product is not of interest, it is very easy to detect this quickly. If, on the other hand, the product is interesting, you may have spent one of the most profitable five minutes of your life.

There are some other areas which provide cost reduction opportunities with some slogging.

INCOTERMS

The International Chamber of Commerce first developed their International Commercial Terms (INCOTERMS) in 1936, with the aim of defining uniform rules for the interpretation of trading terms.

These have subsequently been updated in 1953, 1967, 1976, 1980 and 1990, to take account of new methods of transportation and lately advances in communications technology, e.g. Electronic Data Interchange (EDI).

Function of INCOTERMS

The prime function of INCOTERMS is: 'To determine at what point the seller has fulfilled their obligations so that the goods in a legal sense could be said to be delivered to the buyer.'

They also have secondary functions to define.

1. The responsibility for providing export and import licences.
2. The responsibility for and the extent of insurance cover.
3. The packing of goods.
4. The nature and type of documents, and responsibility for their own origination.
5. The duties of both parties to notify the other of arrangements made.
6. The duty for checking operations.

Bills of lading/non-negotiable documents and EDI

The bill of lading has traditionally satisfied three functions:

1. Proof of delivery on board nominated vessel.
2. Evidence of existence of carriage contract.
3. Provide a negotiable document permitting sale of goods in transit.

In recent years the use of non-negotiable documents, e.g. 'sea waybills' and 'liner waybills', has increased. Such documents satisfy the purpose of bills of lading insofar as they provide proof of delivery on board and evidence of the existence of the carriage contract.

Such documents, when agreed between the two parties, may be replaced by an EDI message. It should be stressed, however, that under current ICC rules the bill of lading cannot be replaced by a non-negotiable document or EDI message for the purposes of selling goods in transit. Their use should thus be restricted to such contracts where there is no intention for the buyer to sell the goods in transit. It is expected, however, that changes will be made in the rules to provide for the use of EDI for all contracts.

INCOTERMS 1990

The terms have been grouped in four basically different categories.

Group E Departure
This INCOTERM deals with contracts where the intent is for delivery to be effected at the seller's premises.

Group F Main carriage unpaid
Under these INCOTERMS the seller is obliged to deliver the goods to a carrier as appointed by the buyer.

FCA Free carrier.
FAS Free alongside ship.
FOB Free on board.

Group C Main carriage paid
Under these INCOTERMS the seller has to contract and pay for the main carriage of the goods. It is important to note that under Group C terms the seller *does not* assume responsibility to risk in the goods or additional costs incurred after shipment or dispatch.

CFR Cost and freight to port of destination.
CIF Cost insurance and freight to port of destination.
CPT Carriage paid to named place of destination.
CIP Carriage and insurance paid to named place of destination.

The distinction between port of destination and place of destination is drawn to take account of different modes of transport. The CFR and CIF terms should only be applied for sea or inland waterway transportation.

For transport where the ship's rail bears no practical purpose, e.g. roll-on, roll-off or container transport, the CPT and CIP terms should be used.

Group D Arrival
Under Group D, the seller is responsible, and assumes risk in the goods and all costs incurred in delivering the goods to the country of destination.

DAF Delivered at frontier.
DES Delivered ex-ship.
DEQ Delivered ex-quay.
DDU Delivered duty unpaid.
DDP Delivered duty paid.

Summary of ex-works, FOB, CIF and DDP

We list below the salient points from the above four commonly used INCOTERMS. For full reference to these and other terms, you are directed to the ICC INCOTERMS booklet dated 1990.

Ex-works

Under an ex-works (EXW) contract, the seller has fulfilled their obligations to deliver the goods when they make them available for collection by the buyer at the seller's premises. The buyer is responsible for all risks and costs from that point including, but not limited to, loading the goods, transport, insurance, duties etc.

ExW seller's responsibilities

1. Provide the goods and commercial invoice or EDI message in conformance with the contract for sale.
2. Assist the buyer, at buyer's expense, in obtaining any export licence or other official authorization needed for the export of the goods.
3. Place the goods at the disposal of the buyer at the place and time stipulated by the buyer.
4. Bear all risks and costs in the goods up until such time as they have been placed at the disposal of the buyer.
5. Give the buyer sufficient notice as to when and where the goods have been placed at the buyer's disposal.
6. Pay the cost of such checking operations necessary to place the goods at the disposal of the buyer.
7. Pack the goods in a manner required for their transport in so much as the mode of transport is known.
8. Mark packaging in appropriate manner.
9. Assist the buyer, at buyer's expense, in obtaining any documents or EDI messages required for exportation or importation of the goods or for their transit through another country.

ExW buyer's responsibilities

1. Pay the price of the goods as provided for in the contract of sale in accordance with agreed method and credit terms.
2. Obtain at buyer's expense, export and import licences, and carry out all customs formalities necessary for the export, import and transit through another country.
3. Take delivery of the goods as soon as they are placed at the buyer's disposal.

4. Bear all risks and costs associated with the goods from the time they are placed at the buyer's disposal provided the goods have been clearly set aside for the buyer.
5. Pay any additional costs incurred by the seller as a result of the buyer failing to collect the goods once they have been made available for the buyer's collection provided the goods have been clearly set aside for the buyer.
6. Pay all duties, taxes and other official charges associated with the export/import or transit through another country.
7. When entitled by the contract so to do give the seller sufficient notice of time and place of delivery.
8. Pay costs of all pre-shipment inspection, including those mandated for the export of the goods.

FOB (free on board)

Under FOB terms the seller fulfils the seller's responsibilities and obligations when the goods pass over the ship's rail. The buyer is thus responsible for all costs, and risks, from that point. This term may only be used for marine or inland waterway transport, and is not appropriate for containerized or roll-on/roll-off traffic where the FCA term should be used.

FOB seller's responsibilities

1. Provision of goods and commercial invoice or EDI message in conformance with the contract for sale.
2. Obtain at seller's risk and cost such export licences and clearance necessary for the export of the goods.
3. Deliver the goods on board the vessel nominated by the buyer at time stipulated by the buyer and in a manner customary at the port of shipment.
4. Bear all risks in the goods up to the point where the goods pass over the ship's rail at the port of shipment.
5. Pay all costs related to the transport of the goods up to the point that they pass over the ship's rail at the port of shipment.
6. Pay all costs related to export/customs clearance and documentation.
7. Give the buyer sufficient notice that the goods have been delivered on board.
8. Provide the buyer with such documentary proof as defined in the contract for sale of delivery at the seller's expense. Where this is agreed with the buyer this may take the form of an EDI message.

9. Pay the costs of all checking operations for delivering the goods to the vessel for shipment.
10. Pack the goods in a manner required for their transport in so much as the mode of transport is known.
11. Mark packaging in appropriate manner.
12. Assist the buyer, at buyer's expense, in obtaining any documents or EDI messages required for importation of the goods or transit through another country.

FOB buyer's responsibilities

1. Pay the price of the goods as provided for in the contract of sale in accordance with agreed method and credit terms.
2. Obtain at buyer's risk and expense import licence, and clearance necessary for import of the goods.
3. Arrange and pay for onward carriage from port of shipment.
4. Accept delivery of the goods from the time they have been delivered to the nominated vessel at the port of shipment.
5. Bear all risks and costs from the point when the goods have passed over the ship's rail.
6. Pay all costs related to the onward shipment and transport of the goods from the point they have passed over the ship's rail at the port of shipment.
7. Pay all taxes, duties, customs clearance costs and other official charges associated with the import of the goods.
8. Advise the seller, with sufficient notice, of the vessel name, loading point and required delivery time.
9. Accept the documentary proof as defined in contract for sale of delivery provided by the seller. Where agreed this may take the form of an EDI message.
10. Pay, unless otherwise agreed with the seller, all costs associated with pre-shipment inspection unless mandated by the authorities of the country of exportation.
11. Pay all costs incurred by the seller in providing document or EDI messages required for importation or transit through another country.

CIF (cost insurance and freight)

Under CIF terms the seller must pay the costs and freight necessary to bring the goods to the named port of destination and to contract at the seller's expense for marine insurance to cover the buyer's risk of loss or damage during shipment. The risk in the goods passes to the buyer once the goods pass over the ship's rail. The CIF term is not appropriate for container or roll-on/roll-off traffic. For such instances the CIP term should be used.

CIF seller's responsibilities

1. Provision of goods in accordance with the contract.
2. Obtain at seller's own risk and cost such export licences, and clearance necessary for export of the goods.
3. Contract for the onward carriage of the goods at seller's expense, to the nominated port of destination. Such carriage should be contracted for on terms usual for such carriage and should provide for a vessel appropriate for the cargo being shipped following the usual route for such passage.
4. Insure at the seller's expense the goods to be shipped as agreed with the buyer. Such insurance to assign rights to claim in the event of loss to the buyer, or any other person with an insurable interest in the goods. In the absence of advice as to the exact nature of the insurance the seller must contract with insurers of good repute and in accordance with the minimum cover provided for in the Institute of London Underwriters Institute Cargo Clauses to a value of not less than 110% of contract value redeemable in the currency of the contract.
5. Deliver the goods on board the vessel nominated by the buyer and in a manner customary at the port of shipment.
6. Bear all risks in the goods up to the point where the goods pass over the ship's rail at the port of shipment.
7. Bear all costs related to the goods up to the point where the goods have passed over the ship's rail at POS (Port of Shipment).
8. Pay the cost of duties, taxes, other official charges and customs formalities necessary for the export of the goods.
9. Give the buyer notice that the goods have been delivered on board the vessel.

CIF buyer's responsibilities

1. Pay the price of the goods as provided for in the contract of sale in accordance with agreed method and credit terms.
2. Obtain at buyer's risk and expense import licence and clearance necessary to import of the goods.
3. Accept delivery of the goods from the time they have been delivered to the nominated vessel at the port of shipment and receive them at port of destination.
4. Bear all risks and costs from the point where the goods have passed over the ship's rail.

5. Pay all costs associated with the carriage of the goods, with the exception of main carriage costs, from the point the goods are delivered on board the vessel at the port of shipment. These costs to include unloading costs, lighterage and wharfage costs.
6. Pay all taxes, duties, customs clearance costs and other official charges associated with import of the goods.
7. Give seller sufficient notice of time for shipping the goods and/ or port of destination.
8. Accept the documentary proof of delivery as defined in the contract of sale provided by the seller. Where agreed this may take the form of an EDI message.
9. Pay, unless otherwise agreed with the seller, all costs associated with the pre-shipment inspection unless mandated by the authorities of the country of exportation.
10. Pay all costs incurred by the seller in providing documents or EDI messages required for importation or transit through another country.
11. Provide the seller with information necessary for procuring insurance.

DDP (delivered duty paid)

Under a DDP contract the seller bears all risks and costs, including duties and taxes, associated with delivering the goods to the buyer at a named place in the country of importation. It may be used irrespective of mode of transport.

DDP seller's responsibilities

1. Provide the goods and commercial invoice or EDI message in accordance with the contract for sale.
2. Obtain at seller's risk and expense export and import licences, and carry out all customs formalities necessary for the export, import or transit through another country.
3. Contract, at seller's expense, for all carriage and transport necessary to deliver the goods to the place of delivery.
4. Deliver the goods at the time stipulated by the buyer.
5. Bear all risks in the goods until they are delivered to the buyer.
6. Pay all costs associated with the delivery of the goods to the buyer.
7. Pay the costs of all customs formalities, duties, taxes and other official charges associated with the export/import of the goods.
8. Give the buyer sufficient notice of dispatch of the goods necessary to enable the buyer to accept delivery.

9. Provide the buyer at seller's expense with such documents or EDI message as may be required by the buyer to enable the buyer to accept the goods.
10. Pay the cost of all checking operations necessary for delivering the goods.
11. Pack the goods in the manner usual in the trade to deliver the contract goods.
12. Mark packaging in appropriate manner.
13. Pay all costs incurred by the buyer in rendering assistance in obtaining such documents or EDI messages necessary for the purposes of delivering the goods.

DDP buyer's responsibilities

1. Pay the price of the goods as provided in the contract of sale in accordance with agreed method and credit terms.
2. When requested by the seller provide, at seller's expense, every assistance in obtaining import licences or other official authorization required for the import of the goods.
3. Take delivery of the goods.
4. Bear all risks and costs in the goods from the point where they have been delivered.
5. Bear risks and costs in the goods should buyer fail to take delivery at the agreed time and place notified to the seller, providing that such goods have been clearly set aside for the buyer.
6. When entitled so to do by the contract stipulate the time and place of delivery.
7. Accept delivery documents or EDI messages provided by the seller.
8. Pay unless otherwise agreed with the seller all costs associated with pre-shipment inspection unless mandated by the authorities of the country of exportation.
9. Render the seller, at seller's expense, with any assistance requested in obtaining such documents or EDI messages necessary for the purposes of delivering the goods.

We acknowledge the source of INCOTERMS as ICC Publication Number 460, ISBN 92–842–0087–3.

Even though INCOTERMS help the transfer of ownership, there are still points of interpretation.

1. The duty to provide export and import licences.
2. The nature and type of documents.
3. The extent of insurance protection.

4. The duty to pack the goods.
5. The duty of paying for checking operations.

The importation of goods has to be preceded by the negotiation with the overseas source to agree the INCOTERM and then who will cover items 1 to 5 above.

All of the costs naturally add to the unit cost and it is to the buyer's advantage to attempt to have CIF or DDP as the term borne by the supplier in order to ensure that the final unit cost is competitive.

In fact, it is wise to request all overseas sources to quote at either CIF or DDP in the enquiry.

INSURANCE CLAUSES

There is usually an agent employed by the company and the selection of this agent should be a purchasing responsibility. In the process of selecting the export/import agent, you should ask to see the insurance documents in detail.

The most usual basic insurance clause is to cover the goods being dropped into the sea when loading or off-loading them.

From this, road transport is usually the next clause, covering loss or damage and may include riot, fire etc. However, if the goods are being brought by road and there is no possibility that they would be dropped overside, why pay the premium?

The writer on one occasion was importing goods from West Germany which were being carried across France to Calais by road and then over the Channel via Dover to the destination required. Among the extensive clauses was insurance against being eaten by wild animals. So far as the writer knows, there are no wild animals in the world that can eat 240 lb castings, and certainly even less inhabit West Germany, France and the UK!

So, slogging through insurance clauses can also save money and lead again towards the lowest ultimate cost.

12

PREPARATION OF A CONTRACT

A contract is defined in the *Oxford Dictionary* as a written or spoken agreement, especially one enforceable by law; the document recording it.

In Chapter 3, the order terms and conditions were discussed which form a contract and, in Chapter 9, the agreement (another contract) required to be met between buyer and seller to establish an approved supplier was examined. Both these aspects of purchasing require the two parties, the other being the supplier, to agree to certain courses of action and each also define the rights of both parties in the event of a failure in performance of the contract. In Chapter 10, when it looked as though Able Limited might try to stop production overnight, it was necessary to refer to the draft terms and conditions, (Chapter 3) to see if The Company was protected against this possibility, and while the actions being taken were accepted and protected as within the terms and conditions of the order, there was the suggestion that a full break clause could, with advantage, have been added as an extra clause in the terms and conditions of the order.

This is always the problem in contract writing, writing down what you agree to is easy, what is difficult is envisaging what can go wrong; and what measures, remedies and penalties are applicable in case of failure. There is also always the intellectual problem of allowing the supplier and the buyer the same rights when each wants to feel the advantage in the contract lies with their own company.

THE BREAK CLAUSE (THE RIGHT TO CANCEL)

An example is the double-edged sword of the break clause. What The Company wants is to be in the position to break an agreement when the agreement is no longer in the company's best interest. In the case of *Able Limited* versus *The Company*, it was clear that Able's prices were much higher than those of competition. The Company wanted to resource, but because The Company needed to be supplied until it could re-tool with another supplier, there needed to be a period of grace within which (after The Company had signified its intent to resource) Able would continue to supply The Company's requirements (at the old price).

If the break clause had said, 'In the event of Able Limited not being competitive in price, quality, delivery etc., The Company reserves the right to give Able Limited three months' notice of its intention to resource and during this period Able Limited will continue to supply The Company's requirements'. This would have been great for The Company – but how about Able's position? They would want the same even-handed right to give The Company three months' notice to quit; after all, The Company is trying to buy at the lowest ultimate cost – but Able Limited is trying to sell its output for the highest price it can get and Able may have found a customer willing to pay much more than The Company, and want to take advantage of this opportunity as fast as possible.

In this instance, it could be that The Company would not find a supplier willing to take on Able's work at the current price, or to tool up in three months, and so could be in the position of having no supplier after the three months had elapsed!

What if the buyer agrees to accept a break clause which says, 'In the event of failure, on either side, to honour the terms and conditions herewith, the other party reserves the right to withdraw from the agreement without liability three months after it has announced the intention to do so'?

The buyer is sitting on a time-bomb – because this may not suit the buyer's book at all. There is ever-present the fear that the supplier could 'pull the plug' if the buyer fails to honour the contract in some quite insignificant way – such as paying later than the terms and conditions of the contract have stipulated.

So, the buyer who is writing this clause can extend the period of notice – say to six months – that's more comfortable from a resourcing point of view, if the supplier does pull the plug – but how about if the buyer is totally dissatisfied with the quality and delivery from the current supplier – must the buyer endure six more months of pain, before enjoying the services of the new supplier the buyer has found? (The time is of the essence clause does not remove the problem.)

Of course there is no reason why the buyer could not put into the contract words to the effect that if The Company wants to break the contract it need only give three months' notice, but if the supplier wants to break it, they must give six months' notice of their intention.

But if I were the sales director of Able Limited, I wouldn't accept this inequality – would you?

So, it's back to the drawing board for the buyer, who must list all the reasons why the company would want to break the contract and specify what these are.

1. Failure to meet quality levels. (What levels does the company expect? 100% OK, unlikely, 95% OK? Why should The Company accept 5% that are *not* OK?) Therefore, the specification of what constitutes failure has to be specified.
2. Failure to meet delivery requirements. (What if the supplier misses one delivery? Does this give the right to the company to give the supplier notice to quit?) Specification is again required.
3. Prices must be worldwide competitive. (How can a little press shop in Birmingham know what price a Taiwanese press shop can sell at? Are we talking apples for apples?) Again, specification is required.

LESSER PENALTIES

It is clearly possible, with a great deal of effort, to sweat out what the buyer would consider reasons to want to resource – but surely there are lesser penalties available and remedies for contravention of the contract?

An example of this is Section 40 of the Army Act which, until fairly recently, allowed soldiers to be charged with 'Conduct prejudicial to the maintenance of good order and service discipline'. Under this Act, a soldier sleeping on duty in war-time could be, if found guilty, sentenced to any punishment from a reprimand to being shot! To the best of the writer's knowledge, the death penalty for sleeping on duty was hardly ever applied after 1918 (if at all) and we've had lots of wars since – and uncountable numbers of soldiers, sailors and airmen (Section 40 applied to the three services) nodding off whilst on duty.

Lesser penalties need to be thought through prior to resourcing being applied.

In the instance of Able Limited, the most likely outcome was that after the buyer had discovered that he or she was paying too much and informed the supplier of this fact, Able was given a last chance to quote to keep the business.

The implication of dialogue prior to taking the ultimate action needs to be carefully documented and the remedies to be listed.

CONSTRUCTION OF A DRAFT CONTRACT WITH ABLE LIMITED

The preamble to a contract defines the parties involved and the purpose of the contract. For example:

> The Company contracts to purchase items shown on the attached schedule and any such others as will be mutually agreed to be added later from Able Limited for the duration of their requirement.

Subject to the following conditions:

1. Price

The initial price of these components/items will be mutually agreed on the basis of their content of labour, material and overhead cost expressed as percentages. These costs shall be established on the basis of the operation sheets in use in Able Limited's machine shops and agreed by Purchasing of The Company.

2. Price reviews

These will take place annually on 1 March. Material, labour and overhead movements and their impact on cost since the date of the last review will be presented by Able Limited to The Company not later than 15 January. Able Limited agree to accept The Company's decision to be final as to whether or not price increases will be paid. Any price increases paid will be effective from 1 March each year.

3. Worldwide competitive prices

The Company will continuously survey the worldwide market to establish prices. The supplier will be notified of these prices when they are lower than those furnished by the supplier and the supplier will be given an opportunity to meet or beat the prices. In the event of failure, The Company reserves the right to resource to another source.

4. Quality performance

All items are to be manufactured in line with The Company's drawings and specifications – and whatever other information is supplied by authorized servants of the company.

In the event that material is delivered to The Company which does not conform to these standards will be subject to one, some or all of the following:

(a) Rejected and returned to the supplier at the supplier's expense. No time limit on these rejections is set. Replacement materials must be provided at the company's request.
(b) Material rejected which contains a percentage of acceptable items will (if the company needs it urgently) be 100% inspected and the reject parts only will be returned to the supplier at the supplier's expense.
    The Company will render a debit to the supplier for the labour which has been deployed to carry out the 100% inspection at The Company's labour rate for the staff employed plus 5% handling charge, as well as the freight cost involved in returning the rejects.
(c) The Company reserves the right to instruct the supplier to send the supplier's labour to The Company's premises in order to rework the material – or to rework the material at the supplier's expense using either outside contractors – or using The Company's labour. Costs to be borne by the supplier.
(d) Statistical returns will be made monthly showing the supplier's performance in batches received and batches rejected, expressed as a percentage. Should this percentage be over 2% then The Company will issue a serious warning to the supplier that the quality level must be improved immediately. Should there be no significant reduction in a period of three months, action may, at The Company's initiative, be taken to resource the offending materials.
(e) In the event of field failures during the warranty period, the supplier will undertake all costs necessary to rectify the failures, not excluding:
    (i) travel to and from the site where the failure has occurred;
    (ii) all costs of replacement;
    (iii) rectification of all items in the field which are liable to be similarly affected;
    (iv) all legal costs which are associated with the failure when these can be shown to be within the supplier's responsibility and undertake full responsibility for cases of consequential liabilities.
(f) The supplier warrants all items supplied for a period of two years from the date of first use in the field, replacements will be supported for two years from installation under warranty.

Failure to observe these conditions may result in The Company resourcing if these conditions are not observed within a time span The Company considers reasonable.

5. Delivery

Schedules will be issued on or before the 25th of each calendar month. The supplier on receipt of the schedule has 48 hours to examine the schedule and inform The Company of their ability to meet the schedule – or if the supplier must vary the schedule, to indicate where they must do this.

Provided The Company accept this variation, the schedule will be amended accordingly.

From this point, a statistical record will be maintained and analysed monthly by the company, on a batch basis. Each batch will be recorded as late if it does not arrive on the day specified in the schedule. Each incomplete batch will also be recorded. At the end of each month, the supplier will be informed of their score. Anything less than 100% performance will be recorded as 'off standard'.

Repeated failure to achieve 100% performance may be the trigger for resourcing action by the company.

Point 6 can be used for other contract terms specific to any other orders you consider necessary to define.

ARBITRATION

These conditions are quite stringent but govern the discipline the two companies will work under, but what if a disagreement does occur?

For example, if after three years Clause 1 had prevented Able getting a price increase at all due to the buyer invoking the whole of the clause at each review date, what recourse has the supplier? Clearly the supplier could invoke the 'even-handed' break clause – but let us imagine they have been operating at a loss for these three years, surely they have a right to reclaim some of this loss from the company?

The recourse most people think of is recourse to the law – but whose law? English law? Scottish law? French law? This can be very expensive and may be inconclusive. One way round this is to apply English law, but to select a mutually acceptable arbitrator who will mediate according to English law and natural justice.

Both supplier and buyer can agree this point – but again, this requires to be noted as another condition.

On the assumption that the supplier does not accept these conditions and any others not covered in this example, they will refer the contract to their lawyers – as you should already have done with yours, and a negotiation will start. The lawyers can spend months sometimes on this process, so before referring to the lawyers, time should be spent negotiating with the suppliers to try to obtain their agreement before the lawyers are allowed to take an active part in the discussions.

SUPPLIERS' CONTRACTS

Suppliers, of course, normally set out to impose their own contract on the buyer and some of them go to very considerable lengths in order to make the buyer accept the supplier's conditions.

A very common practice is to persuade the chief designer to sign a contract for development, the MD to sign a contract for a new building, the chief production engineer to sign a contract for a new capital machine and so on.

One favourite ploy of lawyers (on both sides) when discussing price is to use a VOP clause — variation of price tied to an index such as the *Monthly Digest of Statistics* (published by HMSO). Their very common belief is that this is an even-handed way of supporting price increases and in most of the contracts which the supplier seeks to foist on the buyer, this clause nearly always figures.

Basically, the HMSO records statistics on cost movements in all industries on a monthly, quarterly and annual basis, and reports them as percentage movements. Thus, if in your industry the growth according to these figures showed a 10% increase year on year, you just cough up your 10% price increase with no argument.

In Chapter 4, it was shown that with a forecast of price increases (which suppliers could justify and in isolation you would agree with) of some 4% it was still possible to end up with the cost of purchases being reduced below zero.

In the writer's experience, the good purchasing department ***never*** pays the increases that the *National Digest of Statistics* reports in its cost growth to industry.

Another favourite ploy of the lawyers writing the supplier's contracts is terms of payment. Typically, with capital machine purchases, the contract will request one-third of the total cost with order, one-third at a mid stage of the construction of the machine and the final third on delivery of the machine to the customer.

This can mean that you will have paid the whole amount for a machine you have been unable to even prove in production! Even cost-wise, this does not make sense because the first third of the total cost is intended to purchase the raw material to build the machine and do the development, the second third is a 'progress payment' and the final third completes the deal.

If a capital machine is going to cost £120 000 and perhaps weighs a tonne, it is unlikely that the material will cost more than say £5000, but you are being requested to pay one-third, i.e. £40 000 up front. Again, the progress payment of another £40 000 usually is requested in these contracts at, say, three months after they have started the machine and three months before it is delivered – at this point, the supplier should be at the stage of machining of the components and the building of the machine. If this is true, they must have *armies* of people in this operation – which again is disprovable.

When a machine is delivered, the customer is expected to pay the final third of the total sum.

The wise buyer will contest each of these conditions because he or she will see that the supplier is aiming at the use of two-thirds of the cost and, at today's high interest rates, is increasing their profit at the buyer's expense and is hoping to be able to deliver the machine – be paid for it and walk away without any subsequent obligation.

The buyer should aim for perhaps 50% at the midway point, perhaps 25% when the machine is delivered and retain the final 25% until the machine has been proved.

SERVICE CONTRACTS (HIRING)

With certain types of office machinery, the contract for hiring the equipment will often contain some real traps for unwary buyers to fall into. One favourite is to write into the contract that the paper will be supplied by the hirer. The prices are often many times the price you would pay from your normal stockist. Another favourite trap is to establish a hire figure such that the equipment is paid for many times over and also, in the event of the customer wishing to terminate the hire agreement early, to pay a very large extra sum in order to do so.

They must not be allowed to have it both ways! Or indeed either way!

It is almost axiomatic that if a supplier offers you a contract, there is a 'con-trick' in there somewhere, so the best advice is to develop your own standard form of contract which is to be read in conjunction with your order terms and conditions, and try in all cases to get the suppliers to accept yours, with appropriate modifications for special conditions.

Establishing a contract is a negotiation in itself, often of more importance than the negotiations discussed in Chapter 10.

CHECK LIST FOR WRITING A CONTRACT

1. Write down what you want to do.
2. Decide how you want to be able to control each action that you wrote down in 1 above (also see Able Limited's contract).
3. Examine the leverage that you have. How much does the supplier want the business? And don't betray how much you need the supplier's business.
4. Consider design rights – patents and copyright.
   Is the intellectual property yours or the supplier's? If it's the supplier's and you want it – how much are you prepared to pay for it?
5. Special tooling. Who pays for it – who owns it?
6. Manufacturing rights after you've finished your requirement. (For example, you have designed something you want the supplier to make on your behalf. If after your requirement was fulfilled – could the supplier sell the product to another customer? If the supplier is not allowed to – what penalties are there you could apply? If the answer is 'Yes, they can', what royalty will you want? How will you monitor these later sales to ensure you get the agreed royalty?
7. The supplier may be selling in competition with you. An example would be oil filters sold as original equipment on vehicles, stocked by the manufacturers in their dealerships for servicing vehicles and also sold by the suppliers to thousands of other outlets.
   How do you control the situation to ensure that the supplier doesn't under-price the product to their outlets so that you make a loss in order to sell your filters through your dealership outlets etc.?
8. Even such things as packaging and shipping need to be agreed in the contract. Consider the INCOTERMS and insurance situation, for example, as described in Chapter 11.
9. Exchange rates (banding). Consider that, at the time of making the original purchase, you are buying a product which costs US$1.75, equivalent to £1.
   If the exchange rate changes to US$2.00 to the £1, your price has gone down in £1 terms – should you argue in your contract that you should be paying less than £1 by a ratio of 2.00:1.75, i.e.

12.5% less? On the other hand, if £1 drops to $1.50, the American supplier could equally argue that since their price was $1.75 they want to be paid 12.5% *more* in sterling terms.

One way to control this situation is by 'banding' where you may agree that provided the change does not exceed 10% either way, there is no change to the $1.75/£1.00 ratio which remains constant.

Beyond that, both parties meet to re-negotiate, or agree that when the 10% band is breached either way, the price is moved only by half the difference etc.

The buyer has to remember that where exchange rates move considerably, an overseas purchase, while highly competitive at one stage in the currency swing pattern, becomes woefully uncompetitive at another. How long is the buyer prepared to bear this?

'Buying ahead' at a certain exchange rate is not really a solution since the company has made a commitment which it must finance by paying interest on what is effectively a loan, in face of the fact that the exchange rate could become more favourable, and they then have to sell the dollars that they bought ahead at a lower price than was paid for them.

10. Health and Safety at Work. Your lawyer will help you in the particular laws which govern your particular contract and must be obeyed, but the Health and Safety at Work and Sale of Goods Act are two that one must pay attention to.
11. Reservation of title (Romalpa). If buying from many countries, you must decide what you will do about a reservation of title clause, which in the UK is often called 'the Romalpa' clause, and in France the 'Reservation du Proprieté'.

    There has been, over recent years, a growing practice of incorporating in contracts for sale 'reservation of title' clauses (often referred to as Romalpa clauses after the first case upholding their utility).

    Some of these clauses are of considerable complexity, and there are many different versions in use, but the essence of the clauses is to reserve the property in the goods to the seller until the price is paid in full, notwithstanding that the goods are delivered to the buyer.

    The purpose of such a clause is, of course, to confer upon the seller some degree of security against the insolvency of the buyer.

    From a functional point of view reservation of title clauses operate like a more extended version of the real rights of lien and stoppage in transit (lien operates while the seller has possession of the goods).

Reservation of title clauses must be expressly inserted; there is no implied real right to reclaim goods from the buyer once they have been delivered merely because the price has not been paid.

In the most straightforward case, the reservation of title clause applies to specific goods which remain identifiable as the goods sold after they have been delivered to the buyer. In law, the clause is not regarded as a mortgage or charge which might require registration, but simply as an ordinary contractual provision deferring the passing of the property until certain conditions have been complied with.

The complications begin when sellers attempt to draft the relevant clause so as to give them security even after the goods have been resold or have lost their identity and been used in the ordinary processes of manufacture.

The reservation of title clause is not intended to prevent the buyer reselling the goods in the ordinary course of business, but it may attempt to transfer the seller's preferential rights from the goods themselves to the proceeds of sale received by the buyer.

It can, however, actually be applied if the customer is significantly late in payment based on the contract terms, you should ensure that this does not appear in your contract.

12. Payment of overseas suppliers. Ideally, one wants to pay at a certain time after the goods have been received in the buyer's factory to protect cash flow. The supplier overseas probably doesn't want to wait that long. There are various ways of ameliorating this problem. One common method is by irrevocable bills of exchange. This is where the buyer lodges a draft with the bank for the value of the next shipment. As soon as the supplier lodges the shipping notes, bills of lading etc. at the bank the money can be drawn by the supplier. But there is a rock in every snowball and even in this very common method of payment there are snags.

    Chief among them is that you have paid for goods – perhaps even before they've been made. When you lodged your draft at the bank and your supplier's bank told the supplier the cash was there, the supplier is able to sell the draft to the bank at a discount.

    Therefore, you need to insert a clause to protect yourself against non-delivery of the goods and to remember the supplier has the use of your money – which is added profit to the seller and is therefore a good reason to *reduce* the supplier's unit price.

Every one of the clauses mentioned in this chapter are clauses you must consider as you prepare the contract. The best piece of advice that you can be given is, boring as it may be, every contract that you see is a snare to be investigated, distrusted and re-negotiated.

Take the offensive, *insist* that you write all contracts and that any contracts suggested by suppliers are referred to you and that no other officer of the company is allowed to sign them but you.

This is another NIMBY problem since many senior managers and directors believe that they have this right, but it saves The Company no end of money, embarrassment and letters from solicitors in the end. So take the bull by the horns.

13

MANAGEMENT BY OBJECTIVES AND MANAGING YOUR BOSS

REVIEW OF OBJECTIVES

When you were given the job of purchasing manager, your boss gave you a series of objectives. Just to remind you, here they are.

1. Supply must be improved.
2. Incoming quality of bought-out materials must be improved.
3. Capital equipment costs must be under better control.
4. Material costs are rising unacceptably.
5. Costs of consumables and non-production are rising unacceptably.
6. Inventory is too high.
7. Our 'contracts' are causing us to get involved in law suits – this must be stopped.
8. Staffing must be adequate to the task.

Methods to attack these problems, measure results and prepare plans to set and achieve objectives have been discussed in the preceding chapters, and you are getting close to the point where each of these objectives can be driven for and achieved.

One important set of measurements now only remains.

You must flow down to your departmental members the objectives that have been laid on you to the extent that they have as much responsibility to perform their jobs to your satisfaction as you have towards your boss.

In the draft job description for the purchasing manager position (Appendix A) is a draft organigram or family tree for the department and the section heads are shown as reporting to you. The job descriptions of the chief buyers contain the functional reporting lines which include the paragraph:

> 'In addition, the chief buyer has a reporting/control function on the section's performance across the range of objectives set/ agreed by the purchasing manager and the chief buyer.'

By selecting and agreeing the appropriate objectives (some of which again flow down to the buyers and purchasing assistants), you are able to function very effectively as a line manager, because by defining the objectives and measuring performance you are in a position to advise, guide, lead and make policy as a direct result of experience gained by the use of this process. As a by-product of the process, you can accurately judge the level of merit award that should be awarded.

These objectives change from year to year (see Chapter 16) and should be 'stretching', but achievable.

As a rule of thumb, an 'excellent' or 'very good' performance should rate a 10% merit, 'good' should attract, say, 7.5%, 'fairly good' not more than 5% and anything below that – nothing except some good counselling sessions. Obviously, if there is no improvement after the counselling sessions, consideration has to be given with regard to the subject's future.

In order that 'excellent', 'good' and other portmanteau words are not devalued, the percentage of the objective achieved should be quantifiable. Also, objectives may be given different weightings.

THE CHOICE OF OBJECTIVES

The chief buyer of the pressing section is one of your direct reports and is the member of staff with the biggest section, so let us examine the objectives you want such a person to achieve.

Objective 1: Improved supply

The methods to use to improve supply are discussed in the procedures in Chapter 6 and in Chapters 7 and 9. The methods boil down to:

1. efficient source selection;
2. reducing the number of suppliers (weeding out the inefficient);
3. recording supplier delivery performance;

4. ensuring that schedules are accurate;
5. ensuring that lead times are accurate;
6. use of consignment/bond stock;
7. approved suppliers' contracts;
8. value analysis, value engineering etc.;
9. ensuring suppliers get paid at agreed intervals.

Judicious choice of these processes will result in an improved supply which can be measured by the reduction of the percentage of shortages that are reported and the number of suppliers that are eliminated. In Chapter 1, Manufacturing and Assembly gave you the number of shortages that they suffered. Let us say that 'job stoppers' were 40 per month and that half of these were pressings, then 20 per month is the figure to aim to reduce.

Expressed as a percentage of total deliveries, this might be 2.5% of deliveries so that a 97.5% delivery on time figure is under-emphasizing the degree of bad supply.

Therefore, improvement of supply should be measured in three ways:

1. say, 10 inefficient suppliers to be eliminated in the next 12 months;
2. shortages to be reduced by 50%;
3. total delivery performance statistic to be raised to 98.75%.

The authority for verification would be:

1. Accounts department report of number of suppliers removed from ledger by Purchasing;
2. daily shortage reports;
3. computerized supplier delivery statistics.

Objective 2: Incoming quality of bought-out materials to be improved

- Quality assurance via the approved supplier contracting method is discussed in Chapters 1, 9 and 12.
- Statistical reporting of rejects in Chapters 9 and 10.

This fits in with Objective 1, as suppliers may well be eliminated due to their poor quality performance. The real test is the reduction of the number of rejects which quality report and an improvement on the statistic which shows that only 90%+ of suppliers deliver good quality.

Therefore, Objective 2 should be measurable as follows:

1. reduction of number of rejections over the year by, say, 20%;
2. increase of deliveries accepted at point of delivery by 5% (computer statistic);
3. increase of quality assured suppliers by, say, 10%.

Quality control will be strong allies in achieving these objectives and their reports will be adequate proof of the performance level achieved.

Objective 4: Material costs rising unacceptably

Chapters 4, 7, 8, 9, 10, 11 and 12 all refer.

Basically, the forecast in Chapter 4 has to be achieved or bettered and, if it is achieved, The Company requirements will be met.

Therefore, only one objective becomes necessary and this is to ensure that, 'at bottom line', costs of purchasing are held at zero, or better.

The evidence is monthly performance report against forecast and monthly PPV reports.

Objective 6: Inventory is too high

The purchasing spend is £24 million. If the inventory of bought-out materials is £8 million, then the times turn is three. Ideally, the times turn should be 12. That means that at any time, inventory should not exceed £2 million.

This aspect is discussed in Chapters 7 and 11.

The Accounts department report value of inventory each month. A possible aim would be to reduce inventory of pressings by 20% in year one. This will involve much closer inspection of scheduled versus manufacturing performance and may well provide political support for corrective pressures on both Production Control and Manufacturing, the Finance and Accounts departments will be happy to ally themselves with this objective, and may well provide much more precise figures on stocks of items by piece-part level to enable you to zero in on the really troublesome areas of inventory.

The chief buyer then has exactly the same discussions with his or her buyers and may be yet more precise still. Mr A's objectives may include resourcing the work currently carried out by Biggins Limited to A Nother, and to improve the quality of Coggins in three months or resource them, and so on.

The objectives set for the consumables and capital chief buyer, would differ in so far as concentration would be focused on Objectives 3, 5, 6 and 7.

Objective 3: Capital equipment costs must be under better control

How the chief buyer will achieve this is discussed in Chapter 8, 9, 10, 11 and 12.

The first measure is that the chief buyer sees all proposed capital purchases before a commitment is made to any supplier, and eventually getting to the stage where the chief buyer puts out all enquiries and is involved in all negotiations.

This is a real NIMBY battle and perhaps the objective measure for the first year is that all proposed purchases are referred to the chief buyer prior to a commitment being made and who then negotiates all contracts.

The measure for this would be a comparison of the chief buyer's records with all the capital purchases made, showing the chief buyer had written or approved all contracts.

From a standing start, if they were able to get at 80% of all 'contractable items' and negotiate price, this would be a very good achievement.

Objectives 5 and 6

These are operated exactly as the pressing chief buyer's objectives.

These too should be flowed down in exactly the same way as the production chief buyer to the buyer.

Objective 8: Our 'contracts' are getting us into trouble – this must be stopped

Clearly, the capital chief buyer cannot be blamed for what went on before taking over the job, but by the use of his or her negotiating skills (Chapter 10) and contracting skills (Chapter 12), he or she should be able to ensure that no further law suits emerge.

The measure would be no more law suits.

THE PRESSING CHIEF BUYER'S MANAGEMENT BY OBJECTIVE (MBO) MEASUREMENT SHEET

It will be seen that the objectives listed amount to eight only and that only four of your boss's objectives are the responsibility of the pressings chief buyer and team. The capital and consumables chief buyer has objectives covering the others as below:

MANAGEMENT BY OBJECTIVE		Page 1
NAME: ____________	TITLE: CHIEF BUYER PRESSINGS	
PERIOD: March 1993 to February 1994	MANAGER: ____________	
OBJECTIVE	WEIGHTING	ACHIEVEMENT
1. IMPROVED SUPPLY a. Eliminate 10 suppliers. b. Pressing shortages reduced by 50%.		

MANAGEMENT BY OBJECTIVE		Page 2
NAME: ____________	TITLE: CHIEF BUYER PRESSINGS	
PERIOD: March 1993 to February 1994	MANAGER: ____________	
OBJECTIVE	WEIGHTING	ACHIEVEMENT
c. Delivery performance statistic to be improved to 98.75%. 2. IMPROVEMENT OF INCOMING QUALITY a. Reduction of rejects by 20%. b. Deliveries accepted report to be at 95%. c. Increase quality assured suppliers from 40 to 44.		
3. MATERIAL COST REDUCTION Maintain forecast of 0 inflation at bottom line (or better).		
4. INVENTORY REDUCTION Reduction of March inventory figure by 20%.		

The chief buyers then convert these objectives to fit the buyer's particular job roles. The chief buyers review the buyer's performance monthly and they in turn review the sections' performance with you, using their own MBOs as the vehicle for the review.

MANAGEMENT BY OBJECTIVE		Page 1
NAME: ______________	TITLE: CHIEF BUYER CAPITAL AND CONSUMABLES	
PERIOD: March 1993 to February 1994	MANAGER: ______________	
OBJECTIVE	**WEIGHTING**	**ACHIEVEMENT**
1. CAPITAL EQUIPMENT COSTS MUST BE UNDER BETTER CONTROL To see at least 80% of all contractable items and negotiate contracts.		

MANAGEMENT BY OBJECTIVE		Page 2
NAME: ______________	TITLE: CHIEF BUYER CAPITAL AND CONSUMABLES	
PERIOD: March 1993 to February 1994	MANAGER: ______________	
OBJECTIVE	**WEIGHTING**	**ACHIEVEMENT**
2. CONSUMABLE COSTS To be maintained at 0 inflation at bottom line (or better). 3. INVENTORY REDUCTION Reduction of March inventory by 20%.		
4. No law suits in period.		

All the pundits say that no more than 10 objectives should appear in anyone's MBOs, but it is always a useful vehicle to add on one or two personal objectives. These can be designed to eliminate faults – such as the fact that one of the pressing chief buyer's staff comes in late at least once a week. It could well be that the chief buyer should add to Mr A's MBOs, 'lateness must be reduced from last year's figure by 50%' or Miss B who is studying French (for which the company is paying) 'must achieve intermediate standard by January 1994'.

WEIGHTING OF THE OBJECTIVES

Weighting of the objectives is necessary, for clearly the lateness and the language training should not be weighted to the same level as the operational requirements, but failure to achieve them as they have been agreed by the staff member and his/her boss must be significantly weighted.

As an example, let us look at the pressing chief buyer's MBOs. On the assumption that the chief buyer and you agree with the objectives and the percentage that should be achieved, Objective 3 may be considered the most important and carry the highest score, Objective 1 as second highest, and Objectives 2 and 4 equal third.

Thus, you could decide to weight them as follows:

1(a)	10%
1(b)	10%
1(c)	10%
2(a)	10%
2(b)	5%
2(c)	5%
3	30%
4	20%

This weighting totals to 100%. Partial achievement gives a partial score, clearly failure to make an achievement at all results in a zero.

YEAR-END PROCESS

Each staff member writes up his/her achievements in the right-hand column. Thus the pressings chief buyer may have written alongside 1(a) '15 suppliers eliminated' and alongside 1(b) 'pressing shortage reduced by 47%', and so on.

The member of staff then passes the completed report to his/her boss and the year's performance is reviewed in detail and the scores added up by the boss, and expressed as a percentage. The chief buyer should also submit each MBO report on his or her buyers – to ensure that the purchasing manager can be satisfied that they are fair and just assessments of the individual's achievements.

In the annual review, the employee has the opportunity to explain why there was only 47% of the reduction in rejections when the objective was 50%. The manager may feel that the employee could have been a little more industrious or that 47% is so near 50% it's not worth marking the employee down.

Either way, the chief buyer should explain why the score has been given in that way and should comment in writing on the employee's performance.

In the event that the performance is significantly below the objective, the manager should listen very carefully to the employee's explanation. It may be for a very good reason, or it may be that the employee needs counselling, further training or some other action.

This further training/counselling etc. becomes an objective to be achieved in the following year.

This process is a very valuable one in keeping the minds of all employees firmly fixed on the objectives that are so important in maintaining and improving the economic health of the company.

MANAGING YOUR BOSS

Your boss gave you the set of objectives that you are now setting up methods to achieve and will also be looking for your commitment to the achievement of these aims.

Many buyers are too modest for their own good; they are only too aware of Murphy's Law (anything that can go wrong *will* go wrong) so they hate giving commitments in case they fail.

You will have to show that once you've made a commitment, come hell or high water, you achieve the objective, or the reason for failure was completely outside your control.

So in order to show the boss what you're doing, you must present a monthly management report which defines your objectives and the level of achievement to date.

An example of a monthly management report is shown below.

By updating this form monthly, you are able to keep track of your own and your department's progress towards the targets you have set yourself to achieve. You may want to include losses fiscal and full year, and compare the result against savings, or present the result net, but while you are showing successes, the boss should be reasonably well pleased with the appointment.

Any manager has a life very similar to that of a boxer, in so far as he or she is only as good as the last fight and you can never rest on your laurels, so you need too to be innovating change where it is right to do so.

There are two major types of boss (and goodness knows how many permutations in between).

THE MONTHLY MANAGEMENT REPORT

PURCHASE MANAGER'S MONTHLY REPORT													
	JUL	AUG	SEP	OCT	NOV	DEC	JAN	FEB	MAR	APL	MAY	JUN	TARGET
*Economics conceded (fiscal)													0.83% (£199 200)
*Economics conceded (full year)													3.27% (£784 800)
*Savings achieved (fiscal)													1.00% £240 000
*Savings achieved (full year)													4.00% £960 000
*Net achievement (fiscal)													0.27% £ 40 800
*Net achievement (full year)													0.73% £175 200
*Quality acceptance improvem't													From 90% to 95%
Supply improvement													From 97.5% to 98.5%
Inventory reduction													20% from 1 July figure
New suppliers qual assured													From 100 to 110
Suppliers phased out													20
Number of new contracts raised													40

1. * Based on prices ruling at 1 July.
2. £24m turnover.
3. ( ) negative.
4. Purchasing objective to offset all increases and produce net full year saving of £175 200 minimum (fiscal £40 800).
5. Savings from QC campaign, supply improvement, inventory reduction in cash terms will be reported separately.

Type A

This boss is what the Australians call a 'stand-over' – no matter what you want to do, they want to stand over you and watch what you are doing – and either criticize or take it off your hands and make a mess of doing it him or herself.

The way to manage this boss is to make sure they don't find out what you want to do yourself, but give them little jobs to do. It sounds cynical – maybe it is – but it keeps them off your back.

Type B

This type of boss is only too pleased to delegate and believes that this is good management practice. You can thrive under this type of boss – but there is one snag – they will ask you to handle something outside your scope and then want to crucify you if you haven't done it the way they wanted it done. When this is done, just drop the boss a note when accepting the task and a brief note as to what you propose to do.

The only thing that both types are greatly interested in is increasing profit. You can always make more savings than you are currently making if you had more staff, better training, better systems etc. Always make requests for these benefits with a money-tag attached. This has the implication that if you don't give me what I want, you're wasting money which you won't otherwise get.

The boss is in the chair

One of the most dangerous times for purchasing is the production meetings, or staff meetings, where the boss is present as chairing the meeting.

Most meetings of this type are where the boss has determined to bring pressure on a department for a better performance.

Who do they blame for this failure?

Purchasing!

Although it wastes a lot of your time, be sure that you have got all your answers – and something to attack each department with, if needed.

The boss often judges people two ways: first, on performance and secondly on the way they handle themselves in the dog-fights these meetings often become. Many bosses read very little, so long memos leave them cold.

If a manager 'loses face' two or three times in the presence of the boss, that manager is in trouble – make sure it's not you.

If you are in trouble in the meeting, don't blame your staff, don't blame the supplier – both of them are perceived to be under your control and, therefore, you are not doing your job if either let you down. Say rather, 'The supplier was unable to keep the promise', or, 'The supplier couldn't hold to the original price' – keep it neutral. If you say 'Able let me down again' or 'Buyer Jones made another blunder' – you're the culprit, not them. Above all, be brief!

Outside the meeting, you can crucify Able Limited and Jones until the cows come home – in that meeting you're in charge and you will put it right!

Never talk off the record

When you're with the boss, don't say anything 'off the record' because it will be used either against you, or your colleagues, unless you really trust the boss.

If you do comment off the record, you may find the design manager hammering on your door raging that you have said to the boss, 'Our design department couldn't design a cardboard box!'

If you think it's true, the way to show it is another line in your monthly report – 'Designs returned to design department for further work'. This is fact, not 'off the record' opinion, but ensure you tell the design manager what you are going to do the month before you start reporting!

Cultivate allies

The way to survive comfortably, and manage the boss, is by cultivating those departments with whom you have common cause. For example, the Quality Manager wants to get Supplier Quality assurance in across all suppliers; work closely with them to achieve a common objective. The Quality Manager will become a staunch ally. Finance and Accounting have objectives – among them are a good service from Purchasing in terms of reliable and accurate reports from Purchasing to help them do their jobs meaningfully. Co-operate with them and you have two further allies.

Manufacturing is the most powerful ally and if they feel you are doing your level best for them in solving their problems, they too will look on you as an ally.

In the last analysis, you manage your boss via the good opinion your equals have of you, they are your most perceptive critics.

14
LET SLIP THE DOGS OF WAR

THE COMPETITIVE STAKES

It is a fact that, as you start work in the morning in the UK, the German and French buyers have been at their desks an hour before you. And, soon after lunch time in the UK, the East Coast US buyers are getting started. Further, while you're in bed, the Japanese buyers are battling with their suppliers and then the East Europeans get started, and the whole cycle starts again.

Whether or not you have realized this, you are fighting a 24-hour battle with the stakes being your company's survival. Your overseas competitors are as alive as you are to the importance of obtaining lowest ultimate cost in order to flourish in world markets and, of course, in the UK you also have some tough competition who also have the same objective.

So how will you succeed and let someone else take the fall?

Many leaders have confronted a situation as fraught as yours may be and perhaps the most appropriate is the US General Patton's advice which was 'To get there firstest with the mostest'. The 'mostest' in this case is the achievement of the lowest ultimate cost for everything that The Company spends money on.

Your forecast showed you what the effect of UK inflation would have on your prices and your savings plan showed you how to offset these increases.

Now you have your defence strategy in place and you know how to resist a proportion of price increases, and you have an attack strategy in the creation of savings and the aim is to do better than zero inflation in your bottom line of prices paid in the next 12 months.

Napoleon's advice about training was, 'If you can give a regiment an easy victory in their first engagement they'll be unstoppable thereafter'. So you must consider the prioritization of objectives in order to 'get the best value for money'.

PRIORITIZATION

Based on your forecast, which although imperfect – none of us have entirely reliable crystal balls – you can predict when your major suppliers will be looking for price increases.

Three months before you should be launching enquiries among their competitors for their best prices for 100% of the business. You should be paying particular attention to the key items and try to obtain production engineering estimates on these whenever possible.

On receipt of the information received from these two sources, you can be in a position to know how to proceed.

In this first year, deal only with existing competition. Next year your net must be spread much wider.

From this study, you will find out who your best current suppliers are and next year you will be aiming to challenge them.

As each negotiation proceeds you must endeavour not only to control price, but also to try for extra benefits in quality improvement, supply improvement, warranty extension and so on, and to award the most successful with an approved supplier contract.

DELAYING IMPACTS

There is another aspect which may be overlooked in view of the large objectives you have, but where a price increase is inevitable, then a delayed implementation date should be negotiated for. This is more or less standard practice and can be hung upon an agreement such as, 'If you do not improve your quality I am not paying an increase and I must see improvement first', or similar arguments can be argued on imperfect supply or any other matter where you have genuine concern. Or again, it may be that you have a financial argument which you can use to push the date of implementation back.

There are two reasons for this, the first is obvious (lower fiscal impact), the second is to try to spread anniversary dates for price reviews to a time more convenient to you.

From the point of view of fiscal effect alone, it could be that you want to leave settlement dates at the end of the financial year. This gives a low fiscal effect and prices will, in general, remain stable for most of the following year. If it is more convenient to have the same workload of negotiations month by month it makes good sense to have the smaller suppliers evenly spread and only the 'majors' in the last quarter of the financial year.

You have this opportunity – don't overlook it in your planning.

DEFENCE IN DEPTH

Another aspect of these negotiations is that many of the suppliers will want to go over the buyer's head and the chief buyer's head and have one negotiation – just with you!

Politely but firmly tell them that the buyer is the individual that they are to negotiate with and that in case of a 'failure to agree', they should then talk to the chief buyer and only then, if in the case of a second failure to agree, should you be involved.

Of course, there will be times when the buyer is not experienced enough or the account is too big for him or her to handle, when it is the chief buyer's responsibility and, in a few cases, yours.

But you need to spend at least some of your time ensuring that there is efficient pre-planning being carried on and, the objectives purchasing are aiming for, clear in everybody's minds.

So your diary will be a well-used tool.

BRIEFING THE MANAGER

When you find yourself facing a supplier who has battled with the buyer and the chief buyer, and is still persisting in the price increase originally requested, the supplier will want to see you.

You will need a brief from your staff beforehand and ensure that you get it before you see the supplier.

There was a very famous Purchasing Manager of a most prestigious company who would say, 'If you cannot brief me with sufficient detail written on a 5 in × 3 in card – then you don't know what the problem is'.

It took practice, but in fact generations of buyers who worked for him learned how to do it (see figure overleaf).

You may decide to see the supplier alone, and Chapter 10 gave you the four negotiating methods:

1. power and coercion;
2. attitude change involving emotion;

Supplier's name: ______________		Material supplied: ______________	
Annual turnover: ______________			
Last price increase: ______________	Date: ______	Percentage: ____	
This request: ______________	Date: ______	Percentage: ____	

Negotiation position:

3. search for middle ground compromise;
4. trading mutually advantageous concessions.

There are two other methods:

1. logical persuasion;
2. exploring genuine business objectives.

Of course, there is no reason why you cannot use something of each of these methods to gain some concessions – but any time you concede at forecast level or above, somebody, somewhere in purchasing has got to offset what you have conceded in order to achieve better than forecast.

SUPPLIER VISITS

During this wave of negotiations, you will be invited to visit suppliers' works in order to see how they make the products you buy – accept where you can. Don't treat it like a swan-around – take notes and fill out a supplier report (Chapter 11), also take a note of the machines and methods as unobtrusively as you can.

Next year, when you are surveying new potential suppliers at home and abroad, you will find these notes invaluable.

The writer has had the experience several times of seeing that the machine tools used by an overseas supplier, who appeared competitive, were faster than the ones used at home. It was only their better machine tools that had made them more competitive.

If the UK supplier was prepared to buy the same machines and provide the cost reduction – why resource?

During the course of these negotiations, there is often the opportunity to ask the suppliers if they could suggest modifications to the design of the product they make which could be produced at a lower price. Others will offer an alternative which is currently supplied to someone else, and from this set of enquiries you will develop another fruitful source of savings.

ENGINEERING SAVINGS

Many suppliers will be able to demonstrate that a relatively simple modification to design would cut the number of operations by half, while others will point out that the material specified on their products is far too expensive and much cheaper alternatives are available. Rationalization is another opportunity where, for example, bolts of the same thread but different lengths could all be rationalized to one common length.

Another group will offer a competitive alternative to what your current supplier is providing.

All these requests require design engineering to change drawings and test the alternatives offered. Engineering will state that changing the drawing, testing, parts lists, operation sheets and perhaps users' manuals will cost, say, £10 000 and that any change which requires all of these processes will not be looked at unless the saving is more than £10 000 per annum. Don't be put off.

Many changes only require a modification to the drawing and a modicum of testing, while others only need a quick test or another supplier's name added to the drawing, and so on.

Equally, if the change you were recommending did need all the actions design engineering state, then this provides you with a good reason that the prospective supplier reduces their price to provide you with a saving of *more* than £10 000 per annum.

You need to work at this because the majority of design engineers object to what they consider to be back-seat driving. If they are unwilling to help, here are two methods to help to persuade them.

1. Engineering managers and directors always have trouble in justifying their existence. From a top management viewpoint, all they seem to do is create expensive engineering changes and try to frighten the top management into submission by saying in a most portentous way, 'Well, if you don't sanction the change – a certain percentage of our product will blow up once it gets into the end customer's hands.' So the engineers would like to show that they can create savings too.
2. Keep a list of the potential savings that could be enjoyed if

Engineering were prepared to set aside time to back Purchasing's effort – and when it reaches a significant figure, send a memo to the boss, copied to the Engineering director.

Often with both 1 and 2, if you are prepared to credit Engineering with 50% of each saving, and the boss and Finance accept that Engineering are helping to create the saving – it puts Engineering in a new light with top management.

You can be well pleased with the fact that, although you can only claim 50% of each engineering saving, the lowest ultimate cost boundary has been approached a little closer.

Before leaving the subject, testing can be a genuine problem if all the engineering test rigs are going to be occupied on higher priority work. Often, the designers of the alternative product designed it to perform on their own test rigs. Engineering can often inspect the potential supplier's test rig and agree a test programme (if the rig is acceptable to them) and, in fact, the supplier carries out the test programme for design engineering on the supplier's own rig. This, of course, is not paid for by The Company since it is a condition of accepting the supplier that the product is adequately tested.

This is again a contribution to lowest ultimate cost.

FACTORY COSTS SAVINGS (CATALOGUE AND CONSUMABLE ITEMS)

Touched on in several different chapters are the non-production purchases, and although they only account for £3 million, and if you include standard parts, a total of £5 million, there is an absolute goldmine to be exploited here in the drive to achieve the lowest ultimate cost, and the potential yield in percentage terms is often much greater than you will save on the bought-out production materials.

Most factories have stores for all kinds of items:

- Standard parts
- Safety clothing
- Stationery
- Plumbers' and electricians' spares
- Grinding wheels, cutters, drills etc.
- Safety footwear
- Cutting oils
- Small tools
- Toilet paper
- Janitorial materials
- Raw materials
- Lubricants
- Paint
- Laboratory equipment
- Photocopy machines
- Scrap sales
- Computer requirements

In many cases, all the items are requisitioned on a random basis by the store keepers and their assistants in order to keep inventory eating its head off based on a stocking policy decided in the year dot!

In most cases, the aim is to keep a float of around one month. This is $1/12$ of £5 million or £416 000. There are also large areas of stock which are dead. The accountants don't want to write it off – but you may be able to sell it at the current standard and solve everybody's problem.

By the use of the blanket order process, and a weekly call-off basis, the average inventory can be reduced to less than £60 000, i.e. less than a week, and most of the store keepers can be redeployed. Of course, approaching this process needs care and finesse in order not to excite opposition until you are ready to make your presentation.

You will probably have to employ all six methods of negotiation internally because you are really in NIMBY country here. Many requisitioners require items by brand name so that you may find in stores the same material supplied by different suppliers where buying from one only would be the lowest ultimate cost solution.

Each of these battles will have to be fought.

SCRAP SALES

One area which has not yet been covered, which should be a purchasing responsibility, is scrap sales. Scrap can be in several different forms and may include the sale of old machines, structural steel, old forklift trucks etc.

The first form of scrap is often known as 'arisings'. These are the product of machine tools and can be borings, turnings and chips, in various types of steel, aluminium, brass, copper, magnesium etc. Each of these, if segregated and oil-free, have generally a good price on the market and contractors are prepared often to pay above market rate for supplies of these materials. Magnesium is a fire hazard and has to be treated under the guidance of the Factory Fire Precautions Acts, but all the others are relatively straightforward.

If your arisings (which in the main will be soaking in oil) are big enough, you can spin the oil out and reuse the oil, and sell your oil-free turnings and cuttings at a higher price because they are oil-free. Obviously, how this is handled is a typical cost benefit study but again, you are driving deeper into NIMBY territory.

Often all the materials are marshalled and the store keeper calls up a local scrap merchant who takes the material away and pays the company by sending a credit.

The first check you must carry out is to see if the material passed across the weighbridge before leaving the company's premises. If it did, and the load was seen to be 1 tonne of bushy steel turnings, ½ tonne of brass turnings and ¼ tonne of copper turnings, then you can easily work out what you should be paid at market price for the weights supplied.

Scrap dealers are shrewd people and not above avoiding the weighbridge and they may also be giving the store keeper a few pounds to write up the delivery note as 1¾ tonnes of bushy steel turnings.

So, if the material does not cross the weighbridge then your second check is to establish the weight of material which is machined and assess roughly what the arisings should/could be.

Then, to check if your suspicions are correct and there is a wide discrepancy, you must ask Security to telephone you next time the scrap dealer calls and watch the materials being loaded.

It could be that the store keeper is naïve and the scrap dealer is being too sharp, but in any event, no company servant should be put into a position of temptation and you will have to find a new scrap dealer, insist that all materials are categorized, that they do pass the weighbridge, they are inspected by security and so on.

The writer has had personal experience of valuable and attractive materials being sold illegally to a scrap dealer, hidden under steel bushy turnings, month after month, until the stock losses were so great that an investigation had to take place and the ruse was discovered.

With regard to the sale of old machines, clearly if they are in working condition and can be reconditioned, these can be sold at auction, or advertised in the *Engineering Buyers Guide* or similar. Only at the last resort should they be sold as scrap by weight. Inside the machines, there may well be valuable electrical equipment, bearings, copper, brass etc., all of which the scrap dealer will extract and quite possibly sell as near new.

It can even pay to strip the machines down and sell the expensive bits yourself.

TRAVEL SAVINGS

While on the subject of adventures in NIMBYland, another sacred cow that needs investigation is travel. In many organizations personnel, for some reason, administer travel centrally, and in other organizations each department selects its own travel agent and the boss's secretary handles the bookings.

Either solution will work provided Purchasing have selected the agent and all travel expenditure is focused through the one supplier. It is obvious that the travel agent's interest in a client is in direct proportion to the size of the account, but the best travel agents offer some very useful benefits to the traveller.

1. Delayed payment. Normally, agents request payment for air tickets within five days – this is laid on them by the rules of the airlines. By lodging a credit card with the agent, the agent is able to pay on the credit card and you receive the bill from the credit card company.
2. The best travel agents offer discounts across a range of hotels and will (if you require their assistance) help you to negotiate company discounts.
3. If you fly regularly on certain airlines, they can assist you to obtain either discounts or rebates on the cost of the flying done by the company's servants.
4. They will also be able to provide visa and passport services, and vaccination at short notice, meet and greet at most airports, car hire benefits, interpreters etc.
5. They will offer staff discounts for holidays booked with them.
6. They will provide a monthly statement of who went where and spent what.

Having completed such a negotiation, you can compare what last year's travel cost was compared to buying the same travel at the new costs, and claim your saving based on the margin between.

As all these negotiations proceed, you will be building a group of suppliers who have accepted the approved source contract which places duties on them over and above the standard terms and conditions with regard to quality, supply and competitiveness. If you've picked the right suppliers, significant improvements will be evident in all of the bosses' seven objectives.

But, there will be suppliers who will be attractive on price, but are not prepared to accept the extra duties an approved source contract imposes, and their quality and supply leave a lot to be desired.

So you have three choices:

1. research to find a better supplier;
2. ignore the supply and quality problems – and deal short term with them when they arise;
3. try harder to get the supplier to improve.

Don't spend much time on any of the choices but 1. Even if you are having to pay more, this is offset by the improvement in other costs – and your reputation is protected.

THE LITTLE BLACK BOOK

In addition to the forecast of planned savings and potential cost impacts, most buyers keep a little black book. If they don't, try to encourage them to do so and keep one yourself.

In the variety of discussions, negotiations, business meetings and so on, ideas for price reduction or achievement of lowest ultimate cost emerge and these should be recorded.

Sometimes too, after a negotiation has been concluded, the buyer may suddenly remember omitting to press this point, or forgetting this question, or didn't go the last mile. These also should be noted in the little black book.

Again, there are sometimes projects which cannot be approached yet because the time isn't ripe – these should also be recorded. This is essentially a private *aide-mémoire*, but its use is to record possible actions for use later and for use in emergency or for future planning.

SOME BLUNDERBUSS TECHNIQUES

Most of the chapters have dealt with the development and introduction of the finer, more precise, tools available to purchasing, but in the battle to achieve lowest ultimate cost, you may have to use cruder methods to achieve your objective.

1. Rejecting claims. If the claim is clearly ridiculous, not properly supported with appropriate justification, too soon after the last price increase, late (in line with the terms and conditions which require all claims to be submitted one month prior to the operating date they want), then reject them out of hand with a brief note explaining why. In the case of the late claim, you can say any subsequent negotiation will only be considered from the date of their communication.
2. Refusal to pay any increase. The simple but steadfast, 'I'm sorry we cannot afford any price increases at all – come and see me again at the start of the new financial year – and I'll see then if there's anything we can do for you!'
3. Very small offer in settlement. 'I can only afford to award you

one-third of your request, although we agree with your justification.'

4. Imposing without the option, say 60 days' payment, from what was originally 30 days.

Items 2, 3 and 4 require a justification which should be true, but they are all effective in their place.

However, blunderbuss methods are the last resort and they have a nasty habit of blowing up in your face later.

With the energy that implementing the programme discussed in the foregoing chapters has generated, you are ready to 'Let slip the dogs of war'. And there is one final move that you might care to make.

During the year you will have awarded quite a few suppliers with approved supplier contracts and these suppliers will be the best you've been able to find to date.

The approved suppliers' conference

One of the ways in which these suppliers will identify themselves more closely with the fortunes of The Company might be to invite them all to a communications meeting.

A typical agenda might be as follows:

1. A welcome from the podium by the MD.
2. A report by you on the improving quality and supply performance.
3. A talk from Marketing/Sales on their sales performance and forward view.
4. If any of your suppliers have achieved zero supply faults and zero quality faults, a special certificate can be awarded.
5. A few words in closing from the MD.
6. Lunch.
7. Guests depart, except for those who opt for the factory tour.

If you wish to spread yourselves further, perhaps for next year you might invite other factory management personnel also to give their input to the occasion.

Although these approved suppliers must be kept worldwide competitive, they are also an extension of the company's operations and you should show that you recognize this.

15

PREPARING FOR THE AUDIT AND LONG-TERM PLANNING

Towards the end of your first year you should be seeing many of the individual objectives and the departmental objectives well on the way to achievement. You believe your people are following your various procedures and policies, and that they are doing their jobs in the way you have laid down.

But are they? Are the disciplines you are demanding being carried out?

THE EXTERNAL AUDITORS

Each year, the company will have the auditors in and, depending on their enthusiasm, they might really turn over Purchasing. Among other things, they look for the 'audit trail', which is that there is a step-by-step traceable trail of paperwork for each purchase. They will look to see if there are areas where Purchasing are leaving areas open for 'fiddling', they will seek to find out if management are slip-shod in the way the departments are run.

Sometimes, they will try very hard to find something adverse to put in their report – even if it is in itself unimportant, because they want to satisfy themselves and their customer – the company – that they have issued a 'fair' report. If they do put in an adverse report on Purchasing, you could be in for a very hard time from your boss!

So don't give them the chance, carry out your own audit!

One process which is used is for the auditor to be armed with a 30 or 40-point questionnaire which will look at all, or some of the following.

1. Purchasing general
   - (a) Position of purchasing in the organization.
   - (b) Role and objectives assigned to purchasing.
   - (c) General statistics produced by purchasing.
   - (d) Objectives within purchasing.
   - (e) Departmental budget.
   - (f) Requisition processes for new components.
   - (g) Timing controls.
   - (h) Key parts.
   - (i) Identification of sources.
   - (j) Cost estimating and cost analysis.
   - (k) Enquiry procedures.
   - (l) Quotation analysis.
   - (m) Authorizations for order placing.
   - (n) Supplier tooling.
   - (o) Orders and order amendments.
   - (p) Sampling and pre-production batches.
   - (q) Material scheduling system.
   - (r) Inventory control.
   - (s) Expediting and delivery performance.
   - (t) Engineering changes.
   - (u) Market testing.
   - (v) Price claims and settlement.
   - (w) Cost savings.
   - (x) Economic forecasting.
   - (y) Supplier rating system.
   - (z) Responsibility for purchasing non-production materials.
   - (aa) Responsibility for purchasing indirect materials, consumables, services and capital.
   - (bb) Disposal of scrap and assets.
2. Interfacing departments.
   - (a) Make versus buy.
   - (b) Quality control:
     - (i) Supplier quality performance.
     - (ii) Supply quality control assessment.
   - (c) Production control.
   - (d) Design engineering.
   - (e) Systems.
   - (f) Finance.
   - (g) Special programme support.
3. Compliance with policies and procedures
   (Sampling.)

4. Appropriateness of organization
   (a) Organization.
   (b) Management style.
   (c) Clerical and administration assistance.
   (d) Workload.
   (e) Professionalism.
   (f) Training.

It will be seen that in section 1, each of the subject headings has been covered by preceding chapters, and represent some of the areas you should consider from the point of view of the audit trail to ensure that your belief is supported by fact.

THE SELF-AUDIT

A quick method whenever you've got an hour to spare is to go to accounts and pick up a fistful of invoices and read them thoroughly.

The things you may find include:

1. buyer signing off price increases without negotiation;
2. price not in line with order;
3. invoices requesting extra costs for delivery;
4. quantities signed off which are different to order;
5. no orders issued;
6. non-approved suppliers in use.

Then go back to purchasing to call for the original orders and compare them with the invoices. Each one of these omissions are ones that the auditors would make a 'big deal' of, so back still further in the trail. Who requisitioned the components? Were they authorized to make the commitment? Was it in their budget?

In the case of the invoice without a supporting order – was a requisition raised – did it go through Purchasing etc.?

Your actions will be determined by what you find, but clearly some people need a shake-up.

With regard to the audit on interfacing sections, the first thing the auditors ask is, 'What sort of service do you get from Purchasing?' It is a question that invites criticism.

The best advice is to make sure that your service to each of these is as correct and efficient as you can make it, because rest assured, there will be criticisms.

When it comes to section 3, the auditors will ask for a copy of your policies and procedures, and then check to see that these are being followed. This is an easy section for you too to audit. You can call for a section of orders through to invoices, checking to see that quotation analyses were prepared, at least three enquiries were raised and that all three suppliers were producers of the component being enquired for etc.

When people know that you are maintaining a perpetual and random audit, they are careful to perform properly, and don't cut corners.

With regard to the appropriateness of the organization, this is where you personally are under scrutiny.

The organization of your department is fundamentally dictated by the balance of incoming work and the structure that you deploy to deal with it. If you're satisfied it works, then you can debate with the auditors any other ideas they have and scotch them or, indeed, listen to them – they could be right.

MANAGEMENT STYLE

Management style is a very personal attribute and literally hundreds of books have been written about it. One piece of advice that sticks in the writer's mind is that which used to be given to Royal Air Force officer cadets as the qualities required of an aircraft captain:

1. empathy;
2. tenacity;
3. efficiency;
4. energy;
5. leadership;
6. personality;
7. rectitude;
8. integrity;
9. courage.

The only one that needs any explanation is empathy. This is the quality of identifying closely with others in order to understand them more closely. Your staff will look to you to display these qualities and they will tend to follow your lead, so you must lead by example in every aspect of your work.

WORKLOAD

If the BSI criteria are adopted, a good working pace is the equivalent of walking at three-and-a-half miles per hour, but you will be driven by other criteria.

1. What is the inflow of work?
2. Are backlogs permissible?
3. How fast should work flow through the department?
4. What improvements are required to cope with the inflow?
5. Is my headcount adequate?
6. In order to process current workload, am I being forced to overlook less urgent priorities which will bite me later on?

This is an area which you should keep constantly under review – for your own sake and that of your department, never mind the auditors.

PROFESSIONALISM AND TRAINING

These two factors are intertwined. Professionalism is the product of good training and good practice.

Each level should be trained to think one level up.

The buyers should be thinking as though they were in their chief buyer's place, the chief buyers should be thinking as though they are in your place and you should be thinking as though you were in your boss's place.

Training people to think this way promotes efficiency and makes a department ready to take on greater challenges because of the reserve of mental ability this promotes.

Again, you have a major role to play here in promoting training and professionalism, and the auditor may want to know just what you are doing about it. This should form a part of each year's plan.

1. How many people do you want to study for the CIPS exam?
2. How many people do you want to learn a foreign language?
3. How many people do you want to put on negotiation training courses?
4. How many would you like to have doing BA or BSc courses in subjects like economics?
5. What level of funding can you support in training in your annual budget?

DEPUTIZING

In order to train people to think 'one level up', a very good method is to let them deputize at meetings. Not only does it widen their view and give them a better understanding of their bosses' responsibilities, it also raises the perception of others about the skills of Purchasing.

Let us say that, normally, the pressing chief buyer attends the Production Managers' weekly production meeting. Each week the chief buyer has to collect data on the promises of material due, the progress of new model items – be prepared to face criticism which may be often unjust and unfair – and still make sure that all the other responsibilities are on stream.

Then the chief buyer decides that one of his or her buyers should attend the meeting instead. The buyer almost certainly will be more seriously savaged than the chief buyer would be – but if the buyer can stand firm and give equal measure, an important training step has been taken, and the buyer will also understand more clearly why the chief buyer drives the buyers so hard to give full and accurate answers to questions.

Gradually, the chief buyer will expose the buyers to the other aspects of the chief buyer's job and the right sort of buyer's performance in his or her own job will visibly improve.

Similarly, the Purchasing Manager should delegate duties for development purposes to his or her chief buyers. This type of training gives the department an extra mobility and flexibility, allowing more people to be absent on company service and still leave a functioning nucleus in operation.

Somewhere around the eighth month of the year, you should be considering next year's objectives and developing a five-year plan.

SALES AND MARKETING'S FIVE-YEAR PLAN

Sales and Marketing will have five-year plans in place. The plan will contain elements of the following:

1. new markets to be opened up;
2. forecast volumes;
3. new model plans;
4. selling price forecasts;
5. profit forecasts.

This plan will be invaluable to you in the construction of your own plan. Most probably, Quality Control, Design Engineering and Mmanufacturing will also have five-year plans, and you need to see how their plans will impact on you because they will not achieve their plans unless purchasing is there too.

1. New markets to be penetrated

As the company expands its sales, the necessity for purchased materials to be at worldwide levels of price becomes increasingly important.

As the world opens up to sales, it must open up to purchasing too. If the new markets are seen to be, say, in the Far East or in Eastern European countries, one of their problems as customers will be scratching together the hard currencies they will need to buy your product.

If they are already selling you components or materials and you are paying them in hard currency, your salespeople will have a much easier job in selling your end product back to them.

This means that next year, as a purchasing objective, you must make very positive studies into these specific new areas to see what products you could buy from them at worldwide competitive prices, while meeting your quality and supply requirements.

2. Forecast volumes

If these volumes are going to change, you need to check your tooling base and suppliers' capacity to see what changes you should make in order to meet these changes when they occur. Do not forget that, if volumes increase, prices should reduce!

3. New model plans

Here you will need to assess what Design Engineering can tell you about the new model requirements. Where they are looking for higher tech black boxes, you should start a potential supplier research programme to get into the position where you are identifying the suppliers that you want development to take place with and presenting these to design as the people that you want to work with.

4. Selling price forecasts

Often, the pricing forecast will start by taking a view of inflation in the markets where the product will be sold and basing the unit prices on the perceived domestic inflation.

They will assume that if inflation in the UK is 5% per annum over the next five years, a Road Burner Mk II will become more than 25% more expensive due to inflation alone during the period of the five-year plan.

They may assume that, since similar views in, say, Germany would result in an inflation of only 3% per annum, the Road Burner Mk II in five years' time would be 10% more expensive in real terms than it is now if sold in Germany.

This argues that in order to keep the price level in Germany over five years you would only be able to concede 3% per annum against a UK inflation forecast of 5% per annum.

But even if our price was to stay level over five years, profit at today's level would have reduced in real terms by 25%.

Therefore, you will have to pay less each year than you do now in order to allow profit to remain the same in real terms over the five years.

With a UK forecast of 5% per annum over the next five years, the reduction in material costs each year must be greater than 5% per annum.

5. Profit forecasts

Marketing will have (probably) considered that they can improve profit by introducing cheap new features which will allow them to sell the Road Burner Mk II at an intrinsically higher price to increase their margin.

Also the introduction of the Road Burner Mk III and Mk IV during the five-year period will assist in this process. You will have to set your stall out to support these extra activities.

6. Quality control five-year plan

Typically they will be planning zero defect campaigns and a reduction of Quality Control headcount as their main aims.

7. Manufacturing five-year plan

They may well want to consider make versus buy, getting the core business more refined, increased robotization and headcount reductions.

As you will see, the opportunity for Purchasing to take a proactive role on each of these seven plans depends, to a lesser or greater degree, on the amount of involvement that you can generate from your own department's activities.

This means that Purchasing must write its own five-year plan and drive it. Out of the Purchasing five-year plan will come next year's objectives.

THE PURCHASING FIVE-YEAR PLAN

1. Exploration of overseas supply sources to establish worldwide price levels and, where appropriate, to source overseas if greater lowest ultimate cost (LUC) advantages can be uncovered.
2. Ensure, by constant review, supplier capacity to be equal to expansion requirements.
3. Research into hi-tech sources to satisfy design requirements.
4. Reduce purchasing prices at LUC, year by year by, say, 5% after offsetting UK inflation impacts.
5. Set up programmes to aim at zero defects on bought-out materials.
6. Set up make versus buy exercises and a study of robotized machine tools in order to guide manufacturing, and improve supply/scheduling/lead times in order to assist in headcount reduction plans.

NEXT YEAR'S PLAN

These broad plans now need setting into time contexts.

Items 2, 4 and 5 will be the basic work of your department, coupled will the supply concern in 6. In a sense, this is the easy part because, while it is not a repeat of this year's activity, it progresses from it.

It means that the plans for LUC reductions have to be well planned, supply performance percentages and quality performance percentages must be tightened again, and your approved suppliers are going to have to work harder.

Items 1, 3 and the other section of Manufacturing's plan (robotization and machine study) will have to be handled differently.

One way to do it is to put these three items into the MBOs (management by objectives) of your chief buyers and yourself, another will be to form small project groups within the department – each chaired by you.

The project group approach requires that, with the overseas sourcing, each selected country is researched, suitable sources uncovered, and the members of the team visit the countries and attempt to find LUC suppliers. A similar process is carried out with robotic machine tools and black boxes. Both Manufacturing and Design will want to be involved in the research, and if you can co-opt on to your project groups (which is the wisest solution) representatives from those departments, these exercises will be very productive.

If you do decide to go it alone – beware of the NIMBYS.

Returning to items 2, 4 and 5, you may feel that your first year's objectives have squeezed a lot of suppliers into a position where they will have to increase prices either on their current items or on the new model items you will source on them.

Now is the time, four months before you must present your next year's plan, to make some further saving decisions.

Will you be able to compress your supply base further still next year or must you now start the research for new suppliers? Probably the answer, depending on the product group, is both – so the research element must start now so that you have a resourcing plan in place before the start of the new financial year – and for this you need to start looking for new sources, surveying them, and getting them ready to compete with existing sources as soon as is feasible.

In Chapter 15, the presentation to all the approved suppliers would have possibly included your necessity to reduce prices (or LUC) by 5% during the next financial year.

It is sometimes very useful, well before any negotiations are being planned, to visit the MDs of your major approved sources and explain to them why your objectives for the next financial year are what they are.

They will also know that you must keep them under pressure to search for the lowest ultimate cost and, if they are willing to co-operate, the chances are that they will succeed in meeting your objectives.

On reviewing your situation for the start of the second year, there are some noticeable differences, chief among them that in Year 1 you have seven objectives, while now, with the six objectives, you have now evolved a blend of the two sets covering every base.

Now all that needs to be demonstrated is that whatever buying team among your company's competition is going to go to the wall, it will never be yours.

Good luck!

APPENDIX A
JOB DESCRIPTIONS

JOB DESCRIPTION

1. Job Title: Purchasing manager

Reports to: Managing director

2. Organization

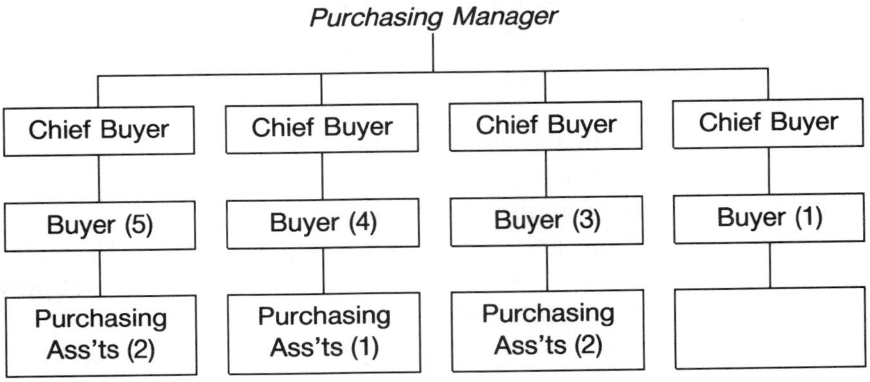

3. Functional reporting lines, other relationships

The purchasing manager is responsible for efficient and effective strategic and tactical sourcing for all commodities, materials and items under manager's control, in order to obtain and maintain a lowest ultimate cost supply organization.

The manager is responsible for cost input statistics to finance, and to provide cost and supply information on projects so requested.

The manager must also maintain close liaison with all departments in the company in order to be able to react through his or her supply chain to any stimulus triggered off by these areas and to keep them informed of developments.

At senior management/director level to take part in long-medium planning/actions to further the company's business objectives.

4. Responsibility for bringing work into the firm

As a by-product of market studies and commercial involvement, the manager will frequently recognize potential profit opportunities that will cause him or her to recommend courses of actions which will result in bringing work into the firm.

5. Manager responsibilities

The 'spend' is £25 million. The manager's prime responsibility is to so manage the affairs of his or her department that this expenditure is made at the lowest ultimate cost to the company. In this regard the manager must:

- target all staff under his or her control to achieve their most effective performance measured on lowest ultimate cost criteria;
- ensure that, by issue of procedures, institution of training and regular audit, that targets are set which, although stretching, are attainable;
- in conjunction with the MD, to agree these targets;
- maintain a continuous study of the various markets to uncover LUC opportunities wherever possible;
- determine strategy and implement, or guide, others to implementation of the tactics necessary in order to achieve supply efficiency at the lowest ultimate cost;
- maintain close liaison with company management to keep up to date with latest long-term strategy and create plans to conform to these requirements;
- development of major supply contracting for future requirements;
- provide costs for incorporation into quotations for submission to potential customers;
- continue to press for company advantage while retaining a position of custodian of the company's image in the market place.

6. Undertaking work

From time to time, the manager undertakes work in the purchasing role as the chief buyer (see chief buyer job description), plus:

Purchasing project work
This is where the purchasing manager develops objectives which aim at lowest ultimate objectives which have not been previously considered, such as:

Value analysis	Supply improvement programmes
Make versus buy	Supplier numbers reduction programmes

Quality improvement programmes
Cost reduction programmes
etc.

Lead time improvement programmes

Extra-territorial market research
Market studies in locations such as the Far East, least developed countries (as well as Europe and North America), where LUC opportunities are uncoverable.

Market advice
Many projects developed outside purchasing can adversely influence arrangements already made by purchasing to the company's commercial disadvantage.

The purchasing manager must be aware of all the countervailing pressures which exist in a commercial situation and be able to comment with authority on the results of precipitate action.

This requires a somewhat philosophical bent in being able to 'see' the chain of events which will stem from any given course of action.

Negotiation support
The targets set by the purchasing manager result in negotiations taking place at lowest levels in the department which may result in the supplier and the junior purchasing representative 'failing to agree'. This may well have been 'pre-planned'.

The purchasing manager is the 'long-stop' in all such negotiations and has therefore to undertake such negotiations effectively. It must also be recognized that if he or she is unsuccessful in arriving at a solution settlement, the manager may be steering towards legal action. This should be avoided, except in exceptional cases, as legal action can call into question the company's commercial attitudes and can damage the company's reputation, as well as being expensive.

7. Innovating

The purchasing manager must, above all, be an innovator. The only way to achieve LUC is by maintaining constant pressure on the market by the widest use of innovative skills.

8. Workflow

The purchasing manager has a very diffuse input of work and to carry out his role, he or she must also travel both domestically and overseas.

Time management is a problem which has to be addressed partly by delegation and partly by good, fast, decision-making skills.

Failure in the manager's ability to make the necessary decisions quickly and accurately can cause very considerable losses to the company.

9. Skills

- Good communicator (foreign languages an asset), written and spoken.
- Analytical skills.
- Persuasive skills.
- Tactical/strategic leadership.
- Psychology of negotiation.
- Commercial law.
- Contracting (UK and foreign).
- Methods of manufacture.
- Labour and overheads.
- QC processes.
- Stores/inventory.
- Procedures.
- Systems.
- Staff control.
- Salaries/rewards.
- Accounting/finance.
- Export/import.
- Currency.
- Shipping.
- Industrial relations.
- Budgeting.
- Planning.

Knowledge of these aspects are obtained by study of the Chartered Institute of Purchasing and Supply Diploma, or BA Business Studies, plus three to four years as a buyer, two to three years as a chief buyer.

The purchasing manager sets the role and ethos of the whole purchasing department and determines impact both on the market and within the company.

Appendix A

JOB DESCRIPTION

1. Job Title: Chief buyer

(Should be read in conjunction with buyer job description)

Reports to: Purchasing manager

2. Organization

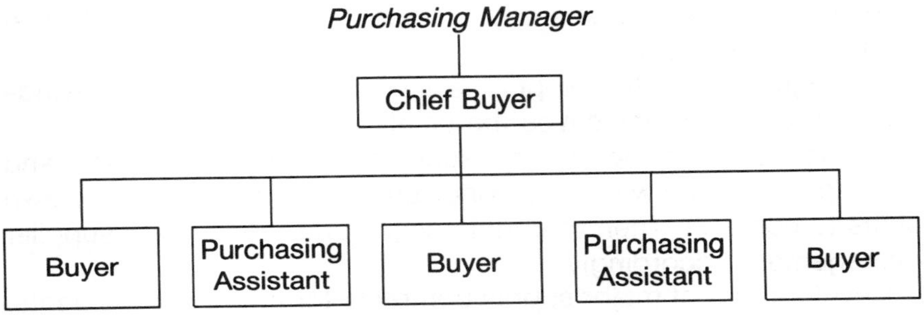

3. Functional reporting lines, other relationships

The chief buyer has the same professional duties as the buyer, but is responsible for the deployment of some £7 million at lowest ultimate cost.

In addition, the chief buyer has a reporting/control function on his or her section's performance across the range of objectives set/agreed by the purchasing manager and the chief buyer.

The chief buyer counsels his or her buyers to achieve their best performance and takes on the most difficult negotiations/supply problems where greater skill and experience are required.

The chief buyer is instrumental in long/medium planning actions, and this involves planning and development meetings with senior levels in the factory and with the suppliers.

The chief buyer recommends purchasing policy and advises, guides and leads his or her section to achieve their optimum performance via 'hands on' and budgetary methods.

All the above are to support projects which are in furtherance of company profit.

4. Responsibility for bringing work into the firm

The chief buyer's objectives are the same as the buyers' but, additionally, with a wider horizon than the buyer, and deploys his or her skills to increase and underpin the buyers' work.

5. Manager responsibilities

To load the buyers under the chief buyer's control to achieve the most effective performance and continued learning/training opportunities.

To determine strategy and to implement the tactics necessary to establish supply efficiency at lowest ultimate cost.

To target buyers on savings objectives ensuring that they are 'stretching but achievable' and to ensure achievement.

To initiate make versus buy studies and to recommend most cost-effective solutions.

In conjunction with the purchasing manager to agree savings and improvement objectives the chief buyer must achieve.

To maintain close liaison with senior company management and to keep up to date with latest long-term strategy, and modify own plans to conform. Then to communicate and to influence supplier management accordingly.

Development of major supply contracts for future requirements. To provide costs to enable estimates to be formulated to be submitted in quotation form to potential customers.

The chief buyer is the highest level in purchasing in normal daily contact with suppliers, and his or her attitudes and decisions are those which represent the company to the outside world of suppliers.

In this, the chief buyer must always press for company advantage without losing the high regard that must be sustained in the market.

6. Undertaking work

The chief buyer works as the buyer plus the following.

Many projects which are developed outside purchasing, for example by design engineering or sales, need input requiring wide market knowledge at an almost philosophical level (rather similar to 'fag-packet' design).

The chief buyer is required to be able to provide this type of information from the depth of his or her experience, based on reading and market knowledge, quickly and often with only minimal time for research.

Co-ordinating the chief buyer's section, often in a hectic environment, is time-consuming; while ensuring simultaneously that section disciplines are maintained and the professional aspects are adhered to. This creates a high pressure deadline driver's climate.

Simultaneously, the chief buyer must maintain measures of efficiency such as management by objective, savings plans, order placing etc.

Market research for materials, product sources which keep the technical aspects of the company at the forefront of technology and 'master-minding' section costing projects are all important parts of the chief buyer's role.

In negotiations to 'role-play' with the buyer, and to stand as the 'big-gun' if the buyer is unable to achieve the planned objectives and to succeed where the buyer cannot.

7. Innovating

In addition to the buyer's role which the chief buyer must also carry out, the senior buyer with his or her wide horizon is well equipped to set up, or recommend, group negotiations to achieve greater benefit to the company – this should be a frequent occurrence.

8. Workflow

The chief buyer shares the same tasks as the buyer but, unlike the buyer, is the initiator of projects aiming at some wider aspect of achieving lowest ultimate cost.

The chief buyer is a decision-maker in many aspects of supplier/supply problem areas since his or her role is to make fast and accurate decisions where failure is measured in unneccessarily high prices paid, or production stopped through lack of components, or when in the estimating role in failure to obtain 'hoped for' business.

9. Skills

- Good communicator (foreign languages an asset), written and spoken.
- Knowledge of markets (domestic and foreign).
- Analytical skills.
- Persuasive skills.
- Tactical/strategic leadership.
- Psychology of negotiation.
- Commercial law.
- Contracting (UK and foreign).
- Methods of manufacture.
- Labour and overheads.

- QC processes.
- Stores/inventory.
- Procedures.
- Systems.
- Staff control.
- Salaries/rewards.
- Accounting/finance.
- Export/import.
- Currency.
- Shipping.
- Industrial relations.
- Budgeting.
- Planning.
- Finance.

These skills are obtained by study of the Chartered Institute of Purchasing and Supply Diploma, or HNC Business Studies, or BA Business Studies, plus three to four years' experience as a production buyer.

The chief buyer role is the 'wheel horse' of the purchasing organization.

Appendix A

JOB DESCRIPTION

1. Job Title: Buyer

Reports to: Chief buyer

2. Organization

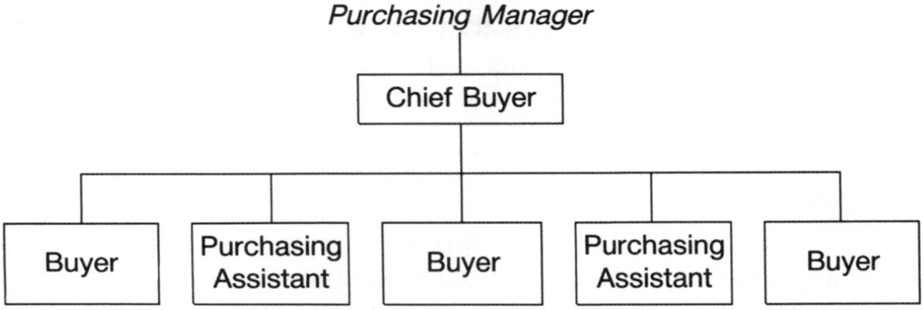

3. Functional reporting lines, other relationships

Each buyer controls an annual turnover approximately £1 million minimum (turnovers vary according to complexity and other factors).

These expenditure responsibilities will cover a range of materials, services and requirements on which the buyer has, or can rapidly develop, speciality market knowledge, both UK and worldwide.

The buyer's objective is to acquire these requirements at the lowest ultimate cost, by identification and establishment of the most effective and cost-efficient suppliers available.

The work comes to the buyer from various departments in the shape of requisitions, production releases etc., and his or her responsibilities include:

(a) establishing lowest ultimate cost for new projects at the quotation stage;
(b) acquire materials, goods or services required for current needs at the LUC via appropriate suppliers;
(c) non-production materials required by end-users;
(d) capital equipment;
(e) prototype materials required by design engineering etc.

In addition to the foregoing, the buyer should maintain contact with:

- quality control;
- production engineering;
- accounting/finance;
- design engineering;
- safety department etc.

The buyer must be *au fait* with their requirements in order to achieve lowest ultimate cost objectives.

The buyer maintains close links with suppliers at all levels within their organizations to ensure that the company is obtaining the requirements from the supplier at lowest ultimate cost.

4. Responsibility for bringing work into the firm

In addition to the buyer's prime objective, which is source selection to provide the company with suppliers who meet the company's needs at the lowest ultimate cost, there is a secondary role, which is to consider where appropriate value analysis, cost analysis, make versus buy can work towards achieving lowest ultimate cost, either with suppliers or within the company.

5. Managerial responsibilities

In certain areas, the buyer will have a small team consisting of an assistant in the form of a junior buyer or a purchasing assistant but, apart from this, the buyer does not normally have managerial responsibility within the company.

Nevertheless, by use of strategic and tactical planning, the buyer manages the efforts of suppliers to meet the prime objective, and also liaises with internal 'customers' in order to help them manage their own functions by suggesting more cost-effective methods in acquiring, and use of, their material and service requirements.

6. Undertaking work

By various requisitioning procedures as outlined in 3, the buyer receives work of varying complexity and urgency, and must show considerable discretion in order that work is dealt within such a manner as to ensure that materials required by the 'customers' are delivered on time.

In order to obtain these at the lowest ultimate cost, the buyer creates a range of initiatives which include:

(a) study of potential/actual economic movements;

(b) study of worldwide markets and commodities;
(c) study of potential suppliers and source selection;
(d) manipulation of markets in order to create leverage with suppliers giving the company competitive advantage;
(e) historic data used to forecast likely future demand.

From these processes which go to create the buyer's market knowledge, he or she then enquires in the appropriate market, negotiating price agreements which meet lowest ultimate cost objectives with the most appropriate and efficient suppliers.

In pursuance of these objectives, the buyer calls regular meetings with suppliers, sometimes at the buyer's premises, sometimes at the supplier's works in order to further his or her projects. In addition, the buyer requires to have regular meetings internally with production control, manufacturing, sales/marketing, quality control, design engineering, accounting, factory management, as well as meetings within purchasing with the staff and management.

7. Innovating

It is axiomatic that there are always further cost benefits which are available.

Methods include:

- material substitution;
- component rationalization;
- improved supply/inventory methods such as bond stock, consignment stock etc.;
- inventory reduction;
- improved supplier performance;
- supplier concentration;
- importation skills;
- currency control;
- use of competition;
- make versus buy;
- supplier liaison;
- contract writing;
- joint developments;
- supplier manufacturing methods;
- value analysis.

The buyer will always be reviewing the foregoing against the range of commodities he or she is responsible for in order to uncover new opportunities.

In this regard, the buyer needs to be at a high level of skill and knowledge which is constantly being improved on:

- commercial law;
- UK/foreign contracting;
- methods of manufacture;
- labour and overhead rates;
- stores/inventory;
- budgeting/planning/finance;
- procedures/systems;
- market knowledge;
- negotiation psychology;
- best course analysis.

8. Workflow

As has already been alluded to in 6, the buyer must always be able to align the expeditious conversion of requisitions into enquiries and then to completed orders, while creating and sustaining an environment of efficient cost-effective suppliers.

This requires good levels of skill in time management and job prioritization in order that the two separate aspects of the buyer's role are harmonized.

The buyer is often required to work to extremely tight deadlines and thus often works under pressure.

9. Skills

The skills listed in 7 are acquired in the Chartered Institute of Purchasing Diploma, or Higher National (Business studies), plus the Purchase Specialities or in BA Business Studies.

This is followed (or in parallel) with experience gained in a purchasing working environment.

After training, a buyer should be proficient in his or her first commodity ranges, in 9 to 18 months the buyer then should be rotated on to other commodity ranges, in 1-year to 2-year cycles, since the wider his or her commodity range experience, the more effective and the more promotable the buyer becomes.

Appendix A

JOB DESCRIPTION

1. Job Title: Purchasing assistant

Reports to: Chief buyer

2. Organization

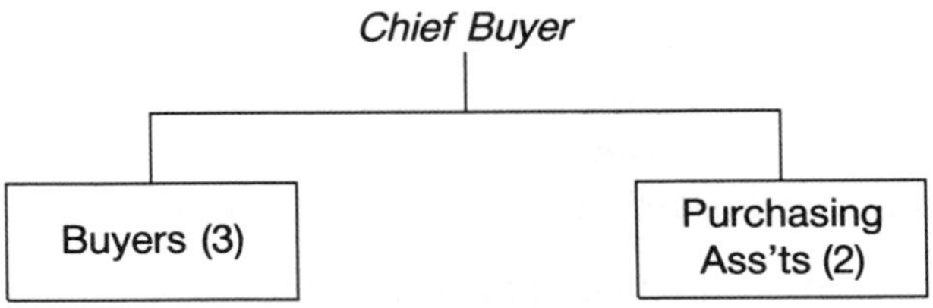

3. Functional reporting lines, other relationships

The purchasing assistant reports to the chief buyer, but also takes instructions from the section buyers.

The purchasing assistant is responsible for the conversion of order drafts and enquiry drafts received from the section buying staff. This may be input work with a computer system or getting them typed (depending on systems in place).

Issuing and dispatching the orders, purchase order amendments and schedules to the required destinations.

The purchasing assistant maintains price records, filing and collects drawings, specifications, photocopying etc., as requested and also compiles lists, analyses and maintains workflow documentation.

The purchasing assistant is also required at times to progress materials from suppliers.

Often, all requisitions and releases are received by the purchasing assistant and logged prior to distribution to the appropriate buyer.

4. Responsibility for bringing work into the firm

None.

5. Managerial responsibilities

None.

Undertaking work

The work requires the ability to:

- organize simple control systems to log incoming and outgoing work and disposition;
- normally VDU inputting skills or cardex type recording;
- maintain
  - supplier records,
  - materials movements,
  - currency movements,
  - correspondence files,
  - issuing of draft orders, enquiries, schedules etc.

After training, the purchasing assistant should acquire a developing skill with facilities such as:

- photocopying;
- printing;
- VDU skills, where applicable;
- also to progress suppliers.

Some correspondence initiated by the purchasing assistant by telephone/fax/memo/letter will be necessary from time to time.

7. Innovating

With the agreement of the chief buyer, the purchasing assistant may develop new systems methods etc.

With training and development the purchasing assistant may be permitted to place orders of low value, and can progress to buyer and above by taking appropriate professional studies, and with experience.

8. Workflow

The first imperative is the emission of orders and enquiries in a timely way from the drafts prepared by the buying staff.

The second is to log, control and allocate work coming into the section, reacting to pre-planned routines.

The third is the preparation of statistics and analyses as requested, and the routine weekly report required by the chief buyer with regard to the work throughput, and the detection of 'bottle necks'.

9. Skills

Since this grade can be used as a training and recruiting ground, a young person with A levels who is prepared to obtain professional qualifications at, say, evening classes, can become an ideal candidate for promotion to buyer rank.

Equally, an older person with BTec (ONC Business Studies) may be suitable. In this latter case, since they may not be candidates for future development, it is advisable not to have too many of this type in the department as they may block promotion opportunities.

APPENDIX B SAMPLE SET OF TERMS AND CONDITIONS OF PURCHASE

1. GENERAL

Except only where expressly agreed otherwise by us in writing, every purchase shall be subject to these printed terms and conditions (thereinafter called Conditions). Any Conditions other than these Conditions and any Special Conditions or Purchase applicable to this Order are expressly excluded. By taking action against this Order you will be deemed to have accepted these Conditions.

2. AUTHORIZATION

We accept no liability for any Goods delivered or services provided unless the Order has been placed or amended on our behalf by a duly authorized officer of the Purchasing Department.

3. PRICES

The price as stated on the order, is fixed, unless otherwise stated or agreed by us. The price includes delivery to the destination stipulated.

4. PAYMENT

Payment shall normally be made against the Supplier's detailed monthly invoice at the end of the month following that month in which the invoice is received, provided such Goods comply with the specification and with the Terms and Conditions of the Order. The payment terms shall only be amended by agreement in writing from the Purchaser. All invoices must be received at the Invoice Point shown overleaf within three days after delivery of the Goods.

5. PACKAGING

You will package the Goods in a manner suitable for transit and/or storage at no cost to us. We will not pay for or return packing materials, unless previously arranged and confirmed in writing.

6. DELIVERY

(a) Time shall be of the essence of this order.
(b) Unless otherwise specified by us delivery of the Goods shall be effected by you at your own risk and expense (including the risk of deterioration in the Goods necessarily incident to the course of transit), at the place and on the date(s) specified in the Order.
(c) In the event of the Goods not being made available on the date(s) specified in the Order we retain the right to cancel the Order pursuant to Condition 11.
(d) We reserve the right to make alternative delivery arrangements and claim an allowance equal to any carriage charge included in your price for the Goods.

7. PASSING OF PROPERTY

The property and risk in the Goods shall pass on delivery or (in the case of delivery instalments) on the delivery of each instalment.

Where the Goods or any part of them though ready for delivery are retained by the Seller pending delivery instructions, then the property in such Goods shall pass to the Buyer upon payment, but the risk in such Goods shall remain with the Seller until actual delivery.

8. INSPECTION AND TESTING

(a) The Goods shall confirm in every respect to the specifications, drawings, samples or descriptions provided or adopted by us, and be free from defects in material and workmanship.
(b) Prior to our acceptance you shall inspect and test the Goods for compliance with the Order and in assessing their fitness for use we shall be deemed to rely on your skill and judgement. You shall, if requested by us, supply certified copies of records of such inspection and tests free of charge. You will grant to us or our nominated representatives a right of access at all reasonable times for the purpose of checking progress and carrying out or witnessing tests and/or inspection procedures. Such tests and inspection as we may carry out shall not in any way diminish, affect or impair your obligations.
(c) Any performance characteristics specified by you in any tender or literature prepared by you or specified in the Contract are of the essence and shall form part of it. You will inform us immediately of any modification affecting the performance or essential specified characteristics of the Goods or any tooling associated with the Goods as found necessary during Commissioning or manufacture. We shall not be bound to accept any modification unless we have agreed to do so in writing.

9. GUARANTEE

(a) Without prejudice of any rights that we may have by statute, common law or otherwise if within 12 months after the Goods have been put into service any defect in the Goods shall be discovered or arise in the normal course of usage, you shall remedy the defect either by replacement or repair at your own expense. You will not be entitled to reject any claim made in respect of any defect arising within the Guarantee period on the basis that we failed to make the complaint during such period.
(b) The provisions of this Clause shall apply to Goods so replaced or repaired and shall be effective from the date of such replacement or repair being put into service but shall not prejudice any of our rights resulting from any defects in the Goods.
(c) If in the case of proprietary goods you give your own specific guarantee or warranty in terms not less favourable than that laid out in condition 9(a), then we shall accept such guarantee or warranty in lieu of condition 9(a). Also, any terms of your

guarantee or warranty which seek to limit your obligation and liabilities under this contract shall be of no effect.

10. DETERIORATION OF GOODS

If the Goods are perishable or have a life expectancy of a fixed duration or if there are any circumstances known to you which would adversely affect the life-span of the Goods you will forthwith advise us in writing of all such necessary and appropriate information relating thereto which shall form part of the description of the Goods.

11. REJECTION AND CANCELLATION

If the Goods do not comply with the Order, or any of the Conditions of the Order are broken or not complied with by you, or it is clear that you will be unable to perform your part of the Order we shall at our discretion be entitled to reject the Goods and/or cancel the Order (notwithstanding that the property in the Goods may have passed) by giving written notice to you and the following provisions shall where appropriate apply.

(a) We shall return to you at your risk and expense any rejected Goods or any Goods already delivered which, by reason of non-delivery of the balance, are not reasonably capable of use by us or at our option shall require you to collect the same.
(b) And we may at our discretion require you either to restore or rectify the Goods to our satisfaction and at your expense or to replace any Goods so rejected upon the same conditions as herein stated.
(c) You will repay to us any money paid by us in respect of rejected or undelivered Goods.
(d) We reserve the right to carry out at your expense such work as may be necessary to make the Goods or any part thereof comply with the Contract.

12. FORCE MAJEURE

(a) We shall not be liable to you for failure to accept delivery of the Goods resulting from any breakdown of plant or apparatus, fire, explosion, accident, picket, strike, lock-out or any other event, or cause beyond our control.

(b) If you fail to perform any part of this Order by reason of any event or cause specified in the preceding sub-clause we may at our discretion suspend or cancel the delivery of the Goods and/or the performance of this Order without any liability to you for payment. In this event we shall also be able to recover from you such sums of money expended by us in connection with the Order.

13. ASSIGNMENT AND SUB-CONTRACTING

You shall not without our written consent assign transfer or sub-contract the Order or any part of it to any third party.

14. CONFIDENTIALITY

(a) This Order and the subject matter thereof shall be treated as confidential between the parties and shall not be disclosed or publicized to any third party for any reason without our prior written consent.

(b) You will not use our name or other identity for advertising or publicity purposes without our prior written consent.

(c) You will not copy, publicize or make available to any third party any drawings, patterns, tooling of any kind, written instructions, specifications and other technical papers supplied by us or produced by you at our cost for the purposes of this Order and same shall remain our property, and must be returned to us on demand free of charge. You will keep safe these items and be responsible for replacing any item lost or damaged in reasonable time and at your cost. You will not modify such items except on our express instructions.

15. PATENTS

(a) Where the Goods are of your design you will indemnify us against any and all liability, loss, damages, claims, costs and expenses arising out of any claim in respect of any infringements of any patent, trade mark, registered design or copyright or other proprietary rights whether in the Republic of Ireland, United Kingdom or elsewhere resulting from your design, manufacture, use, supply or re-supply of Goods.

(b) You will not apply for any Letters Patent or registered Design for Goods supplied against our specifications, drawings, samples or descriptions.

16. INSURANCE AND INDEMNITY

(a) You will insure to their full value any goods, tools, material and any other property provided by or through us to you for your use while they are in your possession or in the possession of any carrier employed by you.

(b) You will indemnify us against all liability loss, damage claims, costs and expenses that arise in respect of the following:
   (i) damage or injury to any persons or property and any other loss or damage arising from any defect whatsoever in the Goods or from any breach by you of any statutory duty or from the acts or omissions of your servants, agents or contractors;
   (ii) your failure to comply with Condition 6.

(c) You shall hold any insurance monies payable under this Clause in trust for us.

17. STATUTORY AND OTHER REQUIREMENTS

You will, in relation to the Goods, comply and it is a condition of this Order that the Goods comply and will continue to comply with the provisions and requirements applicable to the design, manufacture, supply and use of the Goods hereunder whether expressly or by implication or any statute, statutory instrument, order, directive or regulation in force at the time of delivery.

18. BANKRUPTCY OR LIQUIDATION

If you shall become bankrupt or have a receiving order or administration order made against you or shall make any composition or arrangement with, or any conveyance or assignment for the benefit of your creditors or shall purport to do so or shall have any application made against you under any Bankruptcy Act or (being a company) if any resolution shall be passed or an order of the Court be made that you would be wound up (save for the purpose of reconstruction or amalgamation) or a receiver or manager be appointed by any creditor or any act shall be done which would cause any of the foregoing to be done, we shall be entitled to determine the Order by written notice to you but without prejudice to any other right or action which we may have at the date of such notice.

19. WAIVER

No admission act or omission made by us on our part during the continuance of this Order shall constitute a waiver of or release you from liability under any of its terms.

FURTHER READING

Bailey, Peter and Farmer, David, *Purchasing Principles and Techniques*, Pitman for the Institute of Purchasing and Supply.

BSI Buyers Guide, BSI Quality Assurance, P.O. Box 375, Milton Keynes, MK14 6LL.

Drucker, P.F., *The Effective Executive*, Pan Piper.

Farrington, Dr B., *Negotiation Techniques – A Guide to Key Factors*, B. Farrington Limited.

Raven, A.D., *Profit Improvement by Value Analysis, Value Engineering and Purchase Price Analysis*, Cassell Management Studies.

Stuart, Rosemary, *Managers and their Jobs*, Pan Piper.

Sutton, C.J., *Economics and Corporate Strategy*, Cambridge University Press.

Index